Destined for Royalty

Destined
for
ROYALTY

A Brahmin Priest's Search for Truth

LORRY LUTZ

William Carey Library

PASADENA, CALIFORNIA

Published 1986. Second Printing 1987.

Published by
William Carey Library
P.O. Box 40129, 1705 N. Sierra Bonita Ave.
Pasadena, California 91104

ISBN 0-87808-202-6
Library of Congress CIP# 85-22681

Cover design: Evelyn Williams-Brown

Printed in the United States of America

Dedicated to

Charles and Gertrude Bingley

Anand's Canadian foster parents
who loved him as their own son

and to

Wilson and Muriel Flanagan
who cared for the Bingleys in their golden years
as their own parents

I see myself *created by God*
  this helps me to understand
    my size and place in the universe
    my relationship to things and people around me.

I see myself *forgiven by God*
  which makes possible self-acceptance and frees me
  to accept others.

I see myself *called by God*
  which helps me relate what I do to his largest
    purposes and encourages me to do my work as
    well as I can.

I see myself *destined by God*
  which injects a strong dose of hope into my experience
    so that temporary depression can never be
    ultimate despair.

This also means I not only have *ultimate worth*
  but what I do in accordance with God's call
  has permanent significance.

In a sense, I will take what I do with me into eternity
  and offer it as my tribute to God
Who made it possible.

by David Allan Hubbard
President
Fuller Theological Seminary

(used by permission)

Contents

Foreword

When John recorded the fact that Andrew first found his own brother (and said, "We have found the Christ!"), an important tenet of evangelism was laid down. In this volume we have the compelling story of a man who, apart from a painful learning process, wasn't even aware that he *had* brothers—a multitude of brothers—to find.

One part of the book is wryly humorous to me. It relates that silver bells in the family's own beautiful temple would interrupt his boyish play—that they were the signal for elaborate rites of worship which were part of his destiny. *My* play at much the same point in life was "interrupted" by things like the economic necessity of working in cotton fields under a hot Texas sun. At the same time, worship was a subject I viewed with adolescent ignorance and indifference. Such is the variety of the vessels the Lord chooses to dispense His "hid treasures."

I was entirely unacquainted with Anand Chaudhari when the Lord gave Trans World Radio the burden to provide sound, cover-to-cover Bible-teaching for the Hindi-speaking world. But he was highly recommended as translator/speaker for my five-year THRU THE BIBLE series of broadcasts. His daily presentation of the Word has been marked by quiet zeal, obvious compassion, and unusual cross-cultural skill; and the hearts of his vast audience are being won. Now, though still waiting for the joy of a face-to-face meeting, I *know* this man by his "fruits"—the excerpts from his listeners' letters, which reach my office regularly, bring glory to the Lord and warm my heart.

I'm eager for this outstanding story to inspire and motivate its readers. Even more do I anticipate the Unabridged Sequel to be released in the ages to come!

—J. Vernon McGee.

Preface

The taxi driver careened to a stop in front of the aging gas station with the hand operated pumps, to ask directions one more time. We'd been bouncing over narrow rough roads between golden fields of harvested rice, outlined by stately palms wafting romantically in the hot Goanese breeze.

This was the last leg of my research journey to India to put together the pieces of Anand Chaudhari's life. We'd flown from Bombay to Panjim, the capital of the tourist-brochure-looking enclave of Goa, to look for Anand's birthplace.

Once more the taxi driver turned the key, and the Indian "Ambassador" lurched forward. The driver was sure he could find the temple of Durga now. "They said it's just across the river. We'll take the ferry the local farmers use."

The village of Darghal lay hidden off the road in a grove of palms. We parked the taxi and entered the arched gate into the temple courtyard. It was deserted.

Birds sang to each other in the towering palms, and baboons chased each other like children out of school across the veranda roof—but the temple grounds were empty of people.

We stepped carefully through the unkempt grass and found an open doorway into the temple building at the center of the courtyard. The contrast astounded us. A colorful, ornately carved balustrade surrounded the vaulted ceiling. The outer court could have held several hundred people.

Gingerly we entered the inner court. An ancient cart for carrying a goddess, and covered with plastic, was the only furnishing. And above the next set of stairs hung the bells Anand had talked about. I resisted the temptation to sound the gongs.

We removed our shoes before moving up the stairs into the dark windowless inner sanctum. There the silver goddess presided, like a queen in her court, still polished and gleaming after all these years, just as Anand had described her.

Anand had spent his childhood here, hidden away in this village of rural India, with this pagan shrine as the focal point of his life.

But no one is inaccessible when God chooses to use him or her. No one is too far out of reach when our sovereign God destines him for sonship and service.

Today the Rajasthan Bible Institute, which Anand Chaudhari founded, is proof of God's call. RBI evangelists visited one million homes with the Gospel. Sixty thousand have enrolled in Bible correspondence courses; thousands respond to Anand's daily radio programs; more than fifty churches have been planted.

But the miracle of Anand's life is that God plucked him out of Durga's temple in Goa, and thrust him on a path to search for truth that led him to the throne of God.

As I stood looking at Durga's frozen face, a bell shattered the eery stillness, and I turned to see a wizened priest smiling at me, his greying dhoti wrapped around his waist and between his legs. The grubby sacred cord hanging loosely across his chest identified him as a Brahmin priest.

For a moment I thought, "This could be Anand, still offering sacrifices in hopeless rituals."

He would still be there—if God in His sovereignty had not destined him for royalty.

Acknowledgments

A biography of a living person requires that the subject is willing to speak candidly and honestly about himself. I appreciate Anand Chaudhari's cooperation, and the hours and hours of time he gave me. Special appreciation goes to Regina Alexander, Anand's assistant, who really should have been the one to write his story. The final shaping and editing could not have been done without the professional skills of Georgiana Walker, and the careful attention to details of Marilyn Mote and Marty Barclay. And a very warm thanks must go to Jan Schilla, my fellow writer, who pondered the nuances, suggested creative ways to say things, and helped me aim for excellence.

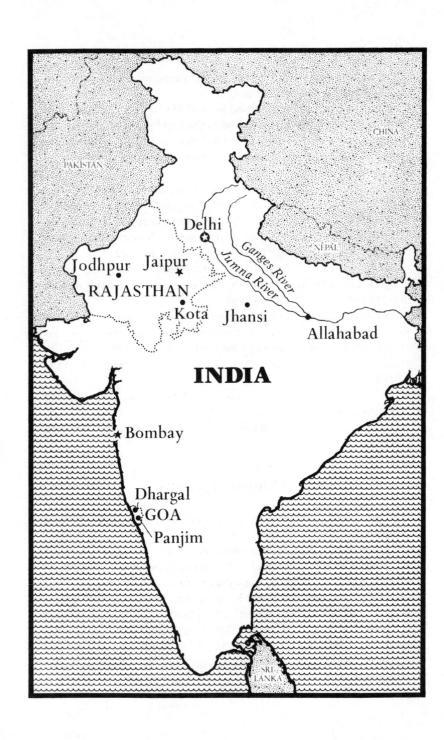

Part I

Durga's Priest
1930-1954

1

The Broken Cord

Anand Chaudhari stepped out of the cool recording studio of the Rajasthan Bible Institute into the searing Indian heat.

He stopped perplexed as he noticed two young men standing near the gate deep in conversation.

"What's Sharma doing here this morning?" he wondered. "He's supposed to be at work."

A premonition swept over him as the two men began walking towards him, though his face showed no emotion.

Anand's Brahmin background had left its mark of discipline. To those who didn't know him he appeared remote—or even haughty. But when he spoke, warmth and concern leapt into his penetrating, deep-set eyes. His eyes, shadowed by bushy dark eyebrows, and framed by heavy glasses, were a window on an alert and insightful mind. "Gentle" best described his crooked smile. His students fondly called their mentor and teacher "Uncle."

Anand smoothed back his thinning grey hair, once wavy and black, which now receded from his finely chiseled face. His thick white sideburns were a sharp contrast to Anand's light brown, wheat-colored skin, which was marred by scattered pock marks.

Anand stood waiting for the two men to reach him, hardly noticing the oven-like heat. Although it was well before noon, soon the temperature would reach over 100 degrees, baking the energy out of man and beast and leaving them wilted and panting for a cool breath. The studio was the only air-conditioned room on the institute's grounds, since the sensitive recording equipment had to be protected from the ravages of moisture and temperature change.

On the far side of the property Anand could see several of the students gathered around an outside water tap, balancing gracefully on their haunches as they splashed the cooling wetness on their faces and over their golden bronze bodies. Their laughter floated towards him over the other sounds of the morning.

He could also hear the cooks talking and laughing as they prepared breakfast out on the open veranda behind his house, skillfully shaping chapatis by slapping them rhythmically against their hands and throwing them onto the pan resting on hot coals.

The clamor of traffic outside the gates of the Rajasthan Bible Institute was a steady noisy commotion. Horns blared with irritation. The whine of bicycle bells clashed with insistent scooter horns, and with the angry calls of oxen drivers moving their lumbering beasts through the morning rush.

The Rajasthan Bible Institute was located on a national highway which passed through the city of Jaipur in Rajasthan, India. The constant movement of people at its doorstep was a reminder of why God had brought Anand Chaudhari here to start a Bible school and to broadcast the Gospel to millions who didn't know who Jesus Christ was.

Sharma had been one of many who'd turned in at the gate to ask questions. But now as he came closer, Anand saw that the usually smiling and cheerful face of the young man was concerned and distraught. It was only a few months ago that Anand had met Sharma for the first time. Sharma had come to RBI after he'd completed one of the Bible correspondence courses. He'd heard about them through Anand's radio broadcast, and had written to enroll.

Anand could clearly remember the day he'd been introduced to Sharma by one the students. "Uncle, Sharma's been studying one of our courses. He doesn't understand some of the things, so he's come to talk with you."

For hours Anand and Sharma had talked together. Anand learned that Sharma was from a high caste Brahmin home in Thoka, nearly seventy miles from Jaipur. He had an excellent job as a legal secretary and had recently married. But there was a great void in his life—a void that the message of the Bible was filling. Before their conversation ended, Anand had been able to answer Sharma's many questions and guide him through the maze of his conflicting Hindu beliefs.

Now as he watched Sharma walking towards him, Anand remembered the last time he'd seen him. The church in Jaipur had scheduled a baptism. When Anand had told Sharma about it, his face lit up with excitement.

"Would they allow me to be baptized too, Uncle?" he'd asked. "I want everyone to know I'm a Christian."

"What will your father say?" Anand had asked. "Are you sure you're ready to face his anger?"

Even though Anand knew this step must be taken, he had seen many new believers fall back into Hinduism when their families discovered they wanted to be baptized. A Hindu could accept that a verbal profession of Christianity was just another step to inner freedom on his path to the nebulous oneness with the cosmos. But baptism was seen as a complete break with Hinduism, and thus an open rejection of what makes an Indian, Indian.

Anand believed Sharma's faith was mature enough for the test, but he wanted to be sure.

"I have to face their anger sometime," Sharma countered. "I love my family—but I must obey Jesus first."

"Besides," he continued, "they're already upset that I don't practice my morning ablutions or pray to the gods at home. They won't even eat with me because I'm considered an outcaste now."

And so one Sunday morning a few weeks ago, Anand had stood in the tank built just inside the front wall of the school compound and watched Sharma step towards him into the water. He was dressed in a pair of slacks and an open-neck shirt. Anand could see that the sacred white triple cord which Sharma had worn since he was initiated as a Brahmin at the age of ten, was gone; the sacred ring was off his finger, and his face was washed and free from ashes and ritual markings.

Sharma had been oblivious of the curiosity seekers who'd stopped to watch the strange proceedings, or even of the brothers and sisters from the Jaipur church who'd gathered for the celebration. As Anand baptized him, he was fully aware of the price Sharma might have to pay, almost wishing he could take his place and bear the brunt of the pain for him.

And now Sharma was back in Jaipur, on a midweek morning when he should have been at work.

As Sharma came near the office, Anand stepped forward and reached out to put his arm around his shoulder.

"What brings you here this morning, Sharma?"

For a moment Sharma stared at him, at a loss for words. But the anguish in his eyes told the story.

Gently Anand asked, "Have they thrown you out?"

Sharma nodded and hung his head. "My wife refuses to come with me. Her parents said they couldn't allow their daughter to live with an outcaste."

Sharma's words were barely audible. "We're expecting our first child—but my parents refuse to let me see her." Then great sobs burst from his throat as he covered his face with his hands.

As Anand gently led the young man into the office where he could be private in his grief, the student who'd accompanied Sharma explained, "That isn't all. Yesterday when he went to work his employer fired him. Evidently the news of his baptism had gotten around town and he said he couldn't afford to have someone with his reputation representing him."

As Anand gave Sharma time to regain his composure, his own heart beat rapidly in his throat. He could feel every pain and understand the agony Sharma was going through. It was as though he were reliving those awful days all over again—the days when he removed the sacred white cord, forever ceased to be a Brahmin, and lost his family.

2

Incense, Candles, and Bells

The bells always rang at dusk.

No matter what Anand and his brothers were doing, the piercing clang of the silver bells ringing through the compound brought their play to a halt. The bells were the signal for worship.

Each evening Anand's father—confident, almost arrogant—would stride into the family temple for the evening ablutions.

To Anand, the temple was the most beautiful place in the world. A balcony with ornately carved and brightly painted wooden railings ran all around the spacious outer court which, on special festival days, was filled with devotees from miles around.

The Shri Santadurga, as the temple was called, was built in the 16th century during the height of the Portuguese inquisition in Goa. Devotees had moved the lavish silver goddess Durga here to Dhargal, a remote village in the middle of lush green rice paddies and stately coconut groves, to keep her from falling into the hands of the Portuguese.

Anand loved to follow his father up the steps into the smaller sanctuary where the goddess was kept inside a barricaded shrine. Only a priest could enter this holiest place to present the beloved goddess with gifts. On either side of the goddess, two brightly-painted gods guarded the holy shrine.

One by one Anand's father would light the candles until Durga, resplendent in hand-wrought silver, seemed to come alive in the dancing flames. The gold and silver objects glowed in the darkening shrine, casting reflections on the gifts of flowers and fruits which the devotees had brought for the priests to place before the goddess. Musicians in the outer court played drums and zithers in honor of Durga, the symbol of power over darkness. Everyone remembered that Durga, Shiva's wife, was sent by her husband to fight the king of the devils. She'd ridden courageously on a lion and defeated the devil. Thus, Durga had become a symbol of power and protection for millions of Hindus.

Here in the temple built to her honor, Anand's father bowed before the goddess. He brought his palms together to his forehead, touching the sacred Naman—two heavy white lines made with sandalwood, reaching from the bridge of his nose to his hairline, and slashed with a center streak of red.

The villagers who gathered each evening for ablutions came to appease the goddess' displeasure or beg her favor. They stood at a respectful distance as the priest began reciting the mantras in a sing-song chant, and poured ghee (clarified butter) over the goddess, watching it run in silky rivulets over her benign face. Then the priest reverently put a garland of marigolds around Durga's neck. Soon the priest's assistant handed him another copper bowl of ghee, which he poured into the sacred fire. As it flared brightly, the smell of burnt oil mixed with the ever-present odor of incense and flowers. All the time the priests continued chanting the mantras in a hypnotic rhythm.

Anand watched his father perform these ceremonies with awe. Even at nine years of age, he knew that as the oldest son, he would one day take his father's place as priest of the family temple and perform all the ceremonies his father did.

When persecution in Kashmir had forced the ancestors of Anand's father's caste to flee from northern India, some members of these Kashmiri Brahmins, considered to be the most respected of the high caste, had settled in Bengal in northeast India, while others had gone to Bangalore.

But one group had traveled thousands of miles across India here to Goa, the Portuguese enclave on India's western coast. That Brahmin subcaste had grown to over 75,000 people, and Anand's father, Sushi Kumar Chaudhari, was priest of one of its three major temples.

Chaudhari was not only a Brahmin priest, the highest level of Hinduism's rigid caste system, but he was well trained. He had studied philosophy and Hinduism for more than twelve years at Benares University, and was a respected pundit in his community. He was called "Shastri," a title given to one who had mastered the Hindu scriptures.

Anand's father was often away on lecture tours for two and three months teaching from the "shastras," the sacred books of Hinduism, some of which dated back several thousand years before Christ.

When he was at home he taught in the temple, sitting cross-legged on a raised dais covered with a clean white sheet. Parents of the village sent their children to be taught the scriptures by him, and Anand would sit with them and listen proudly.

Sushi Chaudhari was a silent man—some might say he was arrogant and proud. As a pundit, he commanded respect as a master guide, with power over his caste community. Any gift from his hand, even water with which he had washed his hands, had merit.

But Anand's father was an "old-type" monk, who did not take advantage of his powerful position in the community. Though the family was cared for by the gifts of the devotees—produce from their fields, profits from sales—the family augmented these gifts from their own garden and a productive coconut grove near the temple compound.

Anand's father was stern and preoccupied with his religious exercises. But his mother, Luxmi, filled their home with warmth and laughter. It was Luxmi who comforted Anand and his four brothers—whose births had followed him in succession every two years, as regularly as the seasons.

Many times Luxmi was called to the bedside of a desperately ill villager, or a dying old woman. She would sit with them through the night, returning in the morning in time for her own prayers and ablutions at the family shrine.

On a few rare occasions Anand heard his father talk about his own childhood. This was usually at special gatherings of the caste when Sushi Chaudhari reminded the people of their history.

"Many of our people settled in Bengal," he would explain. "But others came here and built our temple. My grandfather was a very learned man—people from all over Bengal came to listen to him lecture on the scriptures. My father wanted me to be a great pundit too, so he sent me to the university in Benares."

Anand listened intently, even though he didn't understand everything his father was saying. One thing that puzzled him was why his father had left his family, and never returned to Bengal again.

When Anand pressed his mother for an explanation, she told him, "Your father came to Goa because he couldn't accept his father's view that women couldn't study the scriptures. He believes women should be allowed to study the sacred shastras as well as men."

"Is that why you know so many stories of the gods, Mother?"

Anand interrupted.

"Yes, my son, I learned the sacred scriptures when your father came to Goa to lecture. After a time the caste leaders came to my parents to say that your father was interested in arranging a marriage with me. Since we were from the same background and caste, my parents agreed. When your father returned to Goa to become the priest at this temple, we were married."

The temple and its grounds had been home to Anand since his birth in 1930. His early years were carefree and happy. Anand and his three younger brothers chased each other around the spacious temple compound, which was surrounded by a wall and a continuous veranda with arched pillars. How the boys loved to run up and down the long corridors, or throw stones at the baboons that scampered across the temple roof.

Sometimes they climbed the tower of lights which stood guard outside the entrance to the temple. The most exciting time of year was the festival of lights, when oil lamps were inserted all over the tower. When they were lighted, the tower turned into a magic ladder of lights sparkling into the sky.

Anand and his younger brothers, Sudashiv and Rakesh, often pushed two-year-old Pushpendra away from their games and play, and he would run crying to his mother. A fifth brother, Sidhartha, had recently joined the family. Anand had heard his father proudly declaring that he now had five sons, a sure sign of the gods' blessing.

Anand was glad that the fat healthy baby, suckling so often at his mother's breast, was a boy. After all, his father had said many times that women were born into such a low state because their past lives were evil. They had to live out their karma in this life in obedience and subjection so that perhaps they could return in the next life in the body of a man.

Maybe that was why his mother spent so much time praying before the gods in the special room in the house where they were kept. Every morning before she prepared the family's food or swept the house, Luxmi would kneel before the silver images dressed in colorful costumes, miniature replicas of those in the temple. She repeated long passages of the Hindu scriptures. Every morning she bathed the gods and placed garlands of fresh flowers before them and lit the oil in the brass lamps on the altar.

After she completed her lengthy worship, she prepared her husband's meal, and stood dutifully beside the table while he ate—to make sure that his every wish was met. Anand never saw his mother eat with his father. But when Luxmi's husband had finished eating, she would call the boys to have their morning meal of rice and dal.

Whenever a village leader came to visit Sushi Chaudhari, Luxmi modestly pulled her sari over her heart shaped face with its classical Indian features. Then all that could be seen were her downcast eyes, screened by her heavy black lashes, and the red mark on her forehead to indicate that she was married. No respectable Brahmin woman allowed a man to look her full in the face.

And Anand does not recall his mother ever speaking directly to her husband unless he spoke first. But to the five little boys who took so much of her energy and time, she chattered happily when they were alone. Anand loved those times best, when they squatted around her on the ground as she prepared vegetables or cut up coconuts for their evening meal, and began telling them stories. Sidhartha would be sleeping contentedly on the mat in the corner, and even Pushpendra would settle down with his head on her lap and his thumb in his mouth. He often fell asleep to her sing-song telling, but Rakesh, Sudashiv, and Anand sat enthralled as she embellished the tales of the gods with feats of valour and magical powers.

One of Anand's favorite stories was the tale of "The Boy Gopala and the Child Krishna":

Gopala feared walking through the forest to school each day, so his mother told him that his brother, the Cowherd, would meet him and help him through the dangerous places. Sure enough, each day when he called, "O Brother Cowherd, Brother Cowherd, come and play with me," a boy appeared from the bushes with a little gold crown on his head, with a peacock's feather in the crown.

When Gopala told his mother about the boy in the woods, her heart was filled with gratitude. She wasn't surprised at all. It seemed quite natural that the Child Krishna should comfort his mother's heart.

One day Gopala was asked to bring a gift for the schoolmaster's feast, but his poor mother was sad, for she had nothing to give. Then she brightened up, thinking of the Child Krishna.

"I can't help you," she told her son, "but tomorrow on the

way to school, you must ask your brother in the forest for help."

Gopala did just that, and the Cowherd gave him a little bowl of sour milk—which was one of Gopala's favorite foods. But when he gave it to the schoolmaster, it was so small and insignificant that he hardly paid attention to it. When the teacher noticed Gopala's downcast face, he took the little bowl in his hands and emptied it into a larger one. To his amazement, the little bowl filled right up again. Each time he poured the bowl out, it refilled itself. Then the teacher asked him, "Who gave you this curd?"

Gopala told him of his brother, the Cowherd, in the forest, and the teacher bowed in awe, realizing that the Child Krishna had shown himself to this little one.

As Anand's mother told stories like this one over and over again, Anand learned many of the sacred scriptures which she interwove in the telling. By the time he was nine, he could recite many of the mantras (verses) from the Gita by memory, such as:

"Always think of Me, become My devotee, worship Me, and offer your homage unto Me. Thus you will come to Me without fail. I promise you this because you are My very dear friend." These words had been spoken by the god Krishna, one of the incarnations of Vishnu, to his friend Arjuna in the Bhagavad-gita, an epic Hindu poem. And Anand subconsciously stored this mantra in his memory to use in the future in his own ablutions and worship.

But one day when Anand was nine years old, news came to the temple compound that sent shivers of fear through the family, and was to change his life forever. Several people had come to Anand's father to ask for prayers and offer sacrifice, for members of their families who were very ill.

Now word had come of their deaths—and the dreaded disease was on everyone's lips. Smallpox had struck Goa.

3
Mother Mata's Curse

No one knows how smallpox came to Goa.

Perhaps a Portuguese sailor got off the ship in Panjim with a reeling headache. And before the smallpox symptoms appeared, he could have spread it from bar to bar.

Or an Indian villager from another province may have brought his horrible gift when he came to visit his relatives.

But whatever its source, the smallpox epidemic that swept through the colony of Goa in 1939 was no respecter of persons. It struck poor Hindu farmers and the more affluent Portuguese colonists alike.

For centuries the Portuguese had called the lush, tropical paradise of Goa the "Pearl of the Orient." By 1510, one hundred years before the British East India Company established itself on the subcontinent, the Portuguese already had a toehold on the western coast of India, and began a flourishing trade in the colony of Goa.

They would also be the last Europeans to give up their rights in India; in fact, Nehru took Goa from the Portuguese in a military venture in 1961, bringing to an end more than four hundred years of foreign rule in the tiny enclave.

The early colonizers came with the Portuguese standard in one hand, and a gold cross in the other. St. Francis Xavier, the patron saint of Goa, arrived in 1542, and won a large number of converts to Catholicism. His mortal remains are still kept in the Basilica de Bom Jesus at Old Goa, and are exposed every ten to twelve years to the Catholic devotees. There is little outward difference between the plaster saints enshrined in the cathedrals, and the brightly painted Hindu gods in the temples. Though many claim allegiance to Catholicism, they are bound by superstition and pagan practices of the Indian religions.

But Anand's mother had only condemnation for what she considered the loose living, drinking, and vulgar ways of the Goanese

Christians. Even the word Christian was considered by her to be an abominable thing. Anand himself never met any Christians because his parents kept their family isolated from the contamination of city living.

This resistance applied to all contacts with the Portuguese, including rejection of the medical doctors who practiced in the capital city of Panjim. Most Hindus patronized Indian herbal doctors if they could afford to.

But neither the Portuguese medical profession, nor the Hindu herbalists, were able to stem the terrible smallpox epidemic of 1939.

The Indian strain of smallpox has been long considered the most virulent in the world. Medical authorities believe that smallpox evolved into its final form in India and spread to other countries from there. Though Edward Jenner discovered the smallpox vaccine in the late eighteenth century, the disease was not eradicated in India until May 1975.

In 1939, instead of vaccination to prevent the disease (for there is still no cure), Hindus turned to the goddess Sitala, also known as Mother Mata. Images of Mata show her riding naked atop a donkey, carrying a pitcher and broom in her hand and a basket on her head. Some say the pitcher represents cooling water for the body burning with fever, and the broom is to sweep the smallpox scabs away, or the ashes of the dead bodies she has collected.

As the disease made its way through the villages of Goa, distraught parents came to the temple in Dhargal, bringing offerings for Mata of milk and ghee, pleading with Anand's father to assuage Mata's anger and to ask her to extend her mercy to those dying.

Without realizing it, many Indian mothers followed the best possible course to contain the disease, since vaccination was not yet practiced in this hidden corner of the world. They isolated the sick children in a separate room or in a corner of a one-roomed hut with a cloth hung to cut off contact with others. Leaves of the neem tree were placed over the doorway, to warn those passing by, and no one outside the family was permitted to enter. In an infected village a pole with a red banner was posted outside on the road to turn away travelers.

Yet the virulence of the smallpox in India produced the highest death rate in the world—and the dreaded disease moved inexorably from home to home, striking down primarily children and the elderly, but also many in the prime of life.

Day after day Anand's father was called to say mantras and direct the mourning ceremonies at cremations. The wail of death hung over the village while the smoke and stench of burning bodies filled the air.

Unaware of the fears clutching at their parents' hearts, the little Chaudhari boys played in the temple grounds or entertained their baby brother, just learning to crawl. They didn't understand their mother's stern instructions not to go beyond the gate or to allow other children into the compound to play with them.

But one morning Mata's curse entered the temple grounds— Rakesh woke crying bitterly of pain in his head and back, his teeth chattering from chills that shook his body. Luxmi covered him with blankets and sat with him, terror in her eyes as she saw the telltale symptoms of the dreaded disease.

By the next morning his body burned with fever, his eyes already sunken into his sweet little face. A servant boy was called to fan Rakesh, who was now tossing deliriously on the mat.

Anand and his brothers could hear his incoherent cries as they stood outside the door. They had been commanded not to enter the room; the baby, Sidartha, was being cared for by one of the servant girls, while Luxmi devoted all her time to Rakesh.

By the fourth day, angry red splotches had spread all over Rakesh's body. They had started as painful sores in his mouth and throat, which throbbed and burned so that he cried out in agony for water, only to let it run out of his mouth because it was too painful to swallow.

Luxmi hadn't eaten since her son became ill. She intensified her prayers before the goddess, and Anand's father spent every moment he was not performing ceremonies at the cremations, in the temple reciting mantras, offering gifts and ablutions.

By the end of the first week, Rakesh's body had erupted into hideous wounds. As with the most deadly form of the disease, the pox ran into each other to form huge black pustules which gave forth a noxious odor.

Anand tried to comfort his younger brothers, and even entertained them halfheartedly with some of the games they used to play. But without Rakesh there to join in, it wasn't the same. And then one afternoon Pushpendra woke up from a nap on the veranda complaining of pains in his head and back. Even before his mother could arrange a second mat in the sick room for him, Rakesh, who had been in a coma for several days, stopped breathing, and the terrible death wails began.

Sorrowfully, Anand watched the small body wrapped in a ceremonial cloth being carried out of the compound, his father leading the way back to the cremation site, this time for his own son. He carried a flame burning in a clay bowl, to set the pyre alight. Ordinarily his mother would have followed in the procession, but Pushpendra's deteriorating condition kept Luxmi by his side.

Within a day Sudashiv and baby Sidhartha came down with the fevers, chills and excruciating pains of small pox.

Days and nights ran together as Luxmi vainly tried to stem the progress of the disease. Her own body ached with exhaustion as she bathed Sidhartha's burning body through the night, terrified at the ominous blotches rising on his golden, petal smooth skin. There was no one to help her; the servants themselves had come down with smallpox, or had run away in fear. There was nothing to give Sudashiv and Pushpendra as they tossed in their delirium; nothing to keep them from Mother Mata's anger. Nothing—and one by one Luxmi watched her small sons die, and be carried out of the compound to the funeral pyre.

Sometime during these nightmarish days Luxmi discovered Anand shaking with chills, bravely trying not to cry from the pounding pain that drove his head into his spine. Anand's memories of that awful time are not clear, except that his mother never left his side—day and night—through his pain and fever, the erupting sores that were excruciating to touch, and the agony of trying to swallow past the pox which had become open wounds in his mouth and throat.

In spite of the pain, Anand was fortunate that the sores erupted rather than hemorrhaging under the surface of the skin, a form of smallpox from which no one survived.

One vivid picture stands out in his mind, however. "One night my father sat at my bedside, and seeing my life slipping away, from the depths of his heart he prayed to God—a god he did not even know, Anand recalled.

"I remember that prayer. My father promised that if God would spare me, I would be given to Him for His service. He doubtless meant in the Hindu priesthood, but how differently God answered. For He did hear that prayer, and I recovered."

It was not unusual for the Shastri to speak of a powerful, unknown god. The concept of a universal god is not foreign to Hinduism, in spite of the worship of what some have identified as "330 million gods." In the back of his mind, Sushi Chaudhari believed that somewhere there was a god above all other gods.

But to the Shastri, this god was impersonal, unknowable, beyond imagination or comprehension. Beyond the gods and goddesses represented by the idols, he believed there must be a powerful god who was the ultimate reality. And to this ultimate reality Anand's father dedicated his only remaining son's life.

4

Twice-Born

With the death of his four sons, Shastri Chaudhari was overcome with remorseless guilt and depression. What terrible sins had he committed in his former life to inflict such a heavy karma? How could he do penance and so gain enough merit to expiate the evils of his past life?

Day by day the Shastri became more and more of a recluse. Except for the times when he was called upon to perform his priestly duties, or to supervise Anand's training, Anand's father spent his time reciting mantras, meditating, and practicing yoga.

Through yoga, or meditation, the Shastri believed he could obtain perfection and forgiveness of his sins by removing all thoughts from his mind and concentrating upon the gods. He spent hours sitting motionless on the ground in meditation and controlled breathing. He recited endless repetitions of the mysterious and most powerful monosyllabic mantra, the word "om" or "aum," which represents the supreme spirit, or Brahman himself.

In the weeks of Anand's recuperation following his close brush with death, Anand's mother, now heavy again with another child, devoted all her time and attention to his recovery. The days were long and lonely for Anand without his beloved playmates, and he found himself frequently at his mother's side. He recalls, "Most of the time was spent with my mother, who actually had a great influence upon my life."

But his father did not forget his promise to God at Anand's bedside. Being an honest man of unusual integrity, he now sought to fulfill that promise with meticulous care and dedication.

Another priest was brought into the temple compound to help with Anand's training, and both gave their fullest attention to Anand's studies. Not only were his brothers gone, but village children were no longer permitted on the temple grounds to play with

Anand. The long hours of freedom and boyhood games were forever behind him as he was trained by the two priests.

Before Anand had the right to study the scriptures and share in the daily pujas (sacrifices), and to memorize the sacred mantras (powerful prayers) from the Hindu scriptures, he had to be invested with the sacred triple cord of the twice-born. A Brahmin is superior not only through his high birth, but through this regenerating ceremony (the upanayana), which usually occurs somewhere before the tenth year of his life.

The upanayana is a time of great feasting and festivity, and the heavy cloud of depression seemed to lift from Anand's father for that short period of time. Family and friends were invited from far and near—all Brahmin, of course, since they could not associate with anyone of lesser caste.

Anand watched with excitement as the servants erected a pavilion made of bamboo and coconut mats under which they constructed a special dais. The house and temple were ceremonially cleaned, and long garlands of flowers festooned every room. His mother lovingly bathed the gods and decorated them with fresh clothing and jewels— the family's anger at their failure to protect the dead children abated for the time.

On the first day of the ceremony, Anand sat on the raised platform adorned in colorful new garments and garlanded with flowers. He watched the priest, invited by his father, perform a sacrifice before a small heap of fresh cow dung placed in the center of the pavilion. He offered sandalwood, colored rice, and incense to the god represented by the pungent dung.

The guests were in a festive mood as they were showered with betel nuts, bright colorful cloths and coins, and feasted with mounds of aromatic dishes, served on banana leaves.

On the second day the actual investiture took place. Several Brahmin priests who shared in the ceremony offered "Homam," throwing cooked rice, melted butter and pieces from a fig tree into a pan of hot embers, reciting mantras to consecrate their sacrifices.

Then a barber was brought to the house and Anand went out on the veranda where he cut Anand's nails and shaved his head, except for the sacred tuft at the top, which had never been cut. After this Anand was rushed out to be bathed to remove the defilement of having such a low caste person touch him.

When the sacred moment for investiture came, Anand sat cross-legged on the dais, surrounded by his family, bursting with pride, while the priest placed the sacred triple cord over his left shoulder so that it hung across his chest to his waist. The naman was marked on his forehead—a center line of red with two oblique lines of white were painted on with sandalwood paste. While all this was done, the women sang loudly; outside, musicians played their instruments, bells rang and gongs struck.

Later his father joined Anand on the dais for the highlight of the ceremony. As they both crouched on the floor, a ceremonial cloth was thrown over their heads, hiding them from view of the onlookers. While the musicians played and the women sang, father passed on to son the holy mantras and sacred instructions which the young Brahmin needed to know. Since they were given in Sanskrit, of course, Anand could not understand their meaning yet.

In later years he would realize that the instructions probably included something like this:

"Remember, O my son, that there is only one God who is the Creator, Lord and source of all things; whom every Brahmin should worship in secret. But know also that this is a great mystery that must never be revealed to the vulgar and ignorant people. Should you ever reveal it, surely great misfortune will fall upon you."

With the investiture over, Anand was now ready to go through the arduous training for priesthood. He did not leave the compound to go to school. Rather, the two priests taught him privately hour after hour. It was essential that he learn to read and write so he could study the sacred scriptures—the Vedas, Upanishads, and the epic poems of the Bhagavad Gita and Ramayana.

Since these were written in Sanskrit, he had to learn this ancient language as well as Bengali and Hindi. He also learned arithmetic for calculating propitious days and working out horoscopes.

Anand imitated every move his father made. In the mornings he poured water over his body bare to the waist—even on chilly winter days. Then he modestly removed the wet dhoti wrapped around his waist, by first putting the dry one over it.

Each morning Anand accompanied his father to the temple to perform the sacrifices. He had to be careful to watch his every move, and listen to every word, for if he missed even one detail, the effect was destroyed, and he had to start over again.

Sometimes while his father meditated to prepare for the morning puja, Anand would become restless and disturb his father's intense concentration. Then his father would remonstrate, "Think of the gods, Anand." And he would list the gods in the correct order of meditation.

Some days Anand's father performed the shorter puja so that he could spend time alone in meditation, but on the mornings when the longer sacrifices were offered, father and son could spend two to three hours in the temple. His father would open the heavy barricaded doors which protected the gold and silver gods and goddesses as he began reciting the mantras in a sing-song chant. The main goddess, who was Durga, the wife of Shiva, sat majestically on her ornate silver throne, flanked by two powerful lions. The shrine was lavishly ornamental, but many times as Anand stood dutifully by his father's side, his mind would wander outdoors, wishing he could be running with the village boys, or better yet, playing with his brothers.

The monotonous order of the morning sacrifices placed before the gods had to be strictly followed—water mixed with sandalwood, powdered saffron and flowers; then honey, sugar and milk, followed by water for the gods' bath, a token jewel, some sandalwood powder, then colored rice and flowers. Finally the Shastri lit the incense and the sacred brass lamp and then placed a bowl of cooked food for the gods' needs.

Once the morning ablutions were over, Anand spent much of the day memorizing scripture, under the watchful eye of the priest his father had brought in. Over and over he intoned the Sanskrit words, memorizing hundreds of mantras before he even knew their meaning. To keep him alert, his father often nailed the tuft on the top of his head to a pillar so it would pull painfully if his head began to nod.

One of the first mantras Anand learned was the most famous of all, the gayatri, which only a Brahmin had a right to recite, and then only after he had prepared himself beforehand by other prayers and meditation. The gayatri, a prayer to the sun, is prayed by looking at the sun through the entwined fingers held to the sky:

Ombhur-bhurah-savor
Tat savitar rarenyan
Bhango devasya ahimahi
Dhiyo yonah prachodoyat (om)

It was much later before Anand learned the meaning, which can loosely be translated into English as:

"Let us worship the supreme light of the sun, the god of all things, who can so well guide our understanding like an eye suspended in the vault of heaven." Some priests recite the gayatri as much as 1000 or even 10,000 times a day for remission of sins, or to gain joy, wealth, health and happiness.

Later, Anand would understand that mantras are not synonymous with Bible verses, which are learned to store truth in one's consciousness, and can be called upon for spiritual strength, guidance or comfort. Rather, Hindus use mantras as a magical force to "enchain the power of the gods themselves." Mantras can be used as a preservative or destructive force; an evil spirit can take possession or its effects erased; they can cure or cause illness.

Mantras are the tools of the trade for the successful Hindu priest, who is called upon to perform sacrifices and give powerful mantras to his clients in need. Anand would learn that neither the priest's belief in the power of the mantras, nor even his conviction that the philosophical teachings of Hinduism are true, was critical; the important thing is that the ceremonies are faithfully and correctly carried out, as they have been for thousands of years in the past.

But not all the hours of training and memorizing were monotonous and dull. Anand loved to listen to stories of the incarnations of Vishnu. To many Hindus Vishnu represents the universal god. Anand's mother had told him, "Whenever mankind needs help, Vishnu appears on earth in a reincarnation." Vishnu's most famous reincarnation was Lord Krishna—the prankish child, the amorous adolescent, the hero god. Anand's mother, now suckling his baby sister Pushbanjali, continued telling Anand the stories from the Bhagavad Gita—the famous epic poem and philosophical song about Lord Krishna and the warrior, Arjuna.

He memorized many of the lines from the Gita, such as, "Give thought to nothing but the act, never to its fruits, and let not thyself be seduced by inaction. For him who achieves inward detachment, neither good nor evil exists any longer here below."

Or, "Whatsoever devotee seeks to worship whatsoever divine form with fervent faith, I verily make that faith of his unwavering."

Anand knew many of the legends of Krishna by heart:

The divine Krishna was the eighth child born to Vasudeva and his wife Devaki. The evil prince, Kamsa, had been warned that their eighth child would destroy him, and so he had imprisoned the couple and had all but the first child born to them killed. However, when the baby Krishna was born, all nature blossomed with surpassing loveliness, the stars shone brightly, and Vishnu appeared in miniature form, with four hands and eyes like a lotus flower. His presence lighted up the earth. Once his parents recognized the incarnation, he assumed the form of an ordinary baby. Krishna's father was spirited out of the prison with the infant and exchanged him for a baby girl, whom he brought back. When Kasma heard of the birth he rushed to the prison and dashed the helpless infant against the stone walls, and killed her.

Meanwhile, Krishna grew up as the son of goatherds. He demonstrated unusual strengths. At one stage his foster mother tied him to a huge boulder to keep him out of mischief. Instead, he crawled away, dragging the boulder behind him. When it got stuck between two saplings, he simply uprooted them. Lo and behold, they turned into two humans who had been imprisoned in the trees awaiting their rescue.

The most famous story of Krishna, the goatherd, or Hari, as he was known, was the love of the "gopis," or shepherdesses, for him. So enchanted and bewitched were they by Krishna, that they left their husbands to spend their time playing and making love with him. One story tells of Krishna reincarnating himself 16,000 times so that he could share his love with all the shepherdesses. Meanwhile, back home their husbands did not even know their wives were missing, for Krishna had provided an illusion of them while they were sporting in the forest.

The stories entranced Anand, making the constant study of scripture and poetry somewhat easier. He committed many of the lines from the Gita to memory, never fully comprehending their meaning or being concerned about their truth.

The monotony of memorization and ritual was broken whenever

Anand accompanied his father to perform a puja in the home of a villager. Each family tried at least once a year to call the priest in for a special ceremony. Sometimes it was to thank the gods for a new son, or for a good crop.

Anand looked forward to these ceremonies. As he scurried along after his father, carrying the sacred vessels, he could see his former playmates eyeing him with awe. His heart swelled with pride at the great honor that was his. At these times he almost forgot how lonely he felt in the compound without friends to play with.

When they arrived at their destination, he and his father would sit cross-legged on the floor facing each other. The Shastri scooped out a hollow between them in the floor of mud smeared with cow dung, and laid a sacred fire. The husband and wife and other family members would sit reverently behind them, dressed in their finest. They had been preparing the home for days with ritual cleansing, garlands, and incense for this special occasion.

While his father intoned the mantras, Anand would pour ghee into the flames. Then the family members in turn would repeat the liturgy.

When the ceremony was over, the family presented the priest with gifts, depending upon the family's status. Coconuts and other fruits were common; the more affluent gave money, sometimes a sari for Anand's mother, or a new dhoti for his father or himself. But best of all there were cakes and sweets, and on those occasions Anand was allowed to have all he could eat.

One day Anand's father was called to the home of a villager for a special name ceremony. On the twelfth day after a birth, the priest is asked to prepare a horoscope and give the baby a name.

On this day, as they walked along the road outside the village, a Mohal (an untouchable) passed them, his shadow falling directly in their path. The Shastri jumped back as if struck, but Anand continued forward innocently.

"Look out!" his father shouted. "You've allowed the shadow of the Mohal to fall on you. Don't you know that these people eat dead animals?"

The Shastri jerked Anand back roughly and grabbed the sacred vessel out of his hand. "You've been defiled—and this vessel too."

Anand's father cuffed him on the side of the head, "You know better than this! Now we'll have to go back to bathe before we can proceed with the ceremony."

All the way home Anand received a lecture on the importance of the observance of caste. "Never forget, Anand, that we Brahmins are the highest caste, we came directly from the head of the Creator Brahman. It is to our caste that is given the knowledge of truth and intellectual ability. You must not violate your caste—never eat food prepared by a non-Brahmin; and never, never go near an outcaste. The gods in their wisdom designed the caste system—each caste has its own work to do and its own place to live. Each fulfills its karma as you are yours."

Anand was still too young to understand the complicated caste system which regulated the lives of millions of people. He knew there were four major castes—the Brahmins, or priestly caste; the Kshatriyas, or the warriors; the Vaisyas, the traders or businessmen; and the Sudras, the artisans or craftsmen. Each of these was divided into hundreds of subdivisions.

In later years, as Anand became more aware of the social inequities of India, he realized that caste (which in Sanskrit meant color) was a not-so-subtle form of racial discrimination—actually a scheme by Aryan founders to perpetuate enslavement. The lighter-skinned Aryans made up the higher castes, while the dark-skinned Dravidians from the south were the untouchables or pariahs. As a result, millions of Hindus were locked into a predestined lifestyle, and lifelong predetermined jobs, be it sweeper, garbage collector, or priest. Though Anand was to live to see the caste system officially outlawed in India through the influence of Mahatma Gandhi, who renamed the subcastes Harijans or children of God, the strong social restrictions exist to this day, limiting interaction, intermarriage, and even affecting Christian fellowship.

By the time Anand had gone through the time-consuming purification rituals, bathed, changed into a ceremonially clean dhoti, and walked the long distance back to the villager's home, he had learned his lesson well. The next time a pariah skirted along the side of the street crying out, "Unclean, unclean," Anand doubled the distance between them rather than take a chance at being defiled.

In the rare moments when he did not have to memorize scripture or perform pujas, Anand tried to amuse himself in the lonely temple compound. Sometimes he would throw stones, using trees as target practice, or chase one of the many cats that roamed the compound and had no regard for the sacredness of a rat's life.

One day he found a round wooden ball; it looked as though it had been lying in the grass unnoticed for ages. He began tossing it aimlessly.

Then he saw one of the cats emerge with a new litter of kittens, scampering and falling over each other as they tried to keep up with their mother. Without thinking, Anand aimed the ball at the mother cat. He missed, and instead struck one of the tiny white balls of fluff scampering behind her. Horrified, he saw that the little creature lay unmoving in the dust, blood oozing from its pink mouth.

Anand's mother was just going into the kitchen, her wet sari clinging to her body after her ritual cleansing before she could handle food. When she saw the tragedy she flew at him and shook him.

"What have you done?" You've taken life, son. The gods will have their revenge upon you."

She was almost weeping as she looked upon the blood matted dead kitten, and by now Anand was shaking with fear at the realization of what he had done.

Seeing his shock, Luxmi comforted him. "It's all right. Don't worry. I'll make a sacrifice to appease the anger of the gods."

Anand followed his mother to the door of the kitchen where he was not allowed to enter, and watched her make a thick dough of rice flour and water, kneading it until it was pliable in her hands. Then to his amazement he saw her shape a rough form of a kitten—first the head with two tiny ears, four short legs, and even a tail.

Anand trailed after his mother as she walked over to the temple with the effigy in her hands, and watched her place it before the altar of Durga, bringing her hands together before her face in worship. Then she poured ghee over the tiny figure.

In later years Anand would remember that picture of his mother making a sacrifice for his sins so that he would not have to bear the punishment of the gods.

Day after day, Anand's two years of grueling, tedious, demanding training passed. Then one day news arrived that his mother's sister and husband were coming from Bombay to offer an extraordinary puja, for they had no son to carry on the family. Anand had no idea that this would be the turning point in his life, and start him on a destiny of which neither he nor his father had ever dreamed.

5

A New Life in Bombay

Anand's mother prepared for weeks for the long awaited visit of her younger sister and husband from Bombay. In those days—1942—the trip took 24 hours by train, and another day on a rattly bus loaded to the roof with passengers and produce. So even though his uncle had inherited great wealth, the family did not frequently visit back and forth. Anand had never met his four cousins, but he'd heard his parents discuss the unfortunate fact that they were all girls.

One of the main reasons for this visit was to have the elder Chaudhari offer sacrifices and special ceremonies asking the gods for the gift of a son.

The Bombay Chaudharis (bearing the same name since they came from the same subcaste as Anand's family) did not find the three hundred mile journey or the cost of the extraordinary pujas an unusual price to pay.

It was not unusual to go to great lengths to appeal to the gods for a child. Some have been known to prostrate their bodies on the ground, moving ahead the length of their body in worm-like progress for several miles, until they reach the temple, bleeding and mutilated from dragging themselves over the rough, stony ground. Those who had means, like the Chaudharis, offered elaborate pujas instead.

But during the visit the family became concerned about another problem. Anand recalls his aunt chastising his mother about his lack of schooling. "The boy should be in school, Akka (elder sister). Things are changing in India today, and it is not enough to know the rituals and ceremonies of the temple to get ahead."

Anand's aunt also talked with her husband, and finally a family council was called to discuss his future.

"I'm giving the boy the best possible training for the priesthood," the Shastri defended. "He can read the scriptures in Sanskrit fluently—he has learned mathematics far better than I did at his age."

"But he needs to know more than scriptures, Anna (elder brother)," countered his brother-in-law. "How will he be able to enter the university if he doesn't know English or science? The political scene is changing very fast these days. Mahatma Gandhi's followers are growing, and we may see the British Raj out before we know it. Then there will be even greater opportunities for educated Indians than there are now. You can't prevent your only son from getting the finest education available. Let him come with us so we can put him in the best schools."

Anand's father shook his head and looked for reinforcement from the caste leaders who had joined in for this discussion. The oldest and most orthodox leaders of the caste community had for centuries been called upon to make decisions of importance, and were asked to arbitrate family disputes. On certain occasions they came together to form a court, judging intercaste disputes, and excommunicating those who broke the laws of the caste. Mahatma Gandhi, for example, was excommunicated by his "panchayat," or caste court, for studying law in Britain.

But in this case, the old men, sitting cross-legged on the ground with the rest of the male family members, refused to make a decision, even though they understood why the Shastraji did not want to send his last remaining son to the big city with all its enticements and loose living.

"I've dedicated my son to serving god; here I can be sure that he does not stray from that purpose. He works with me each day, helping me with the ceremonies in the village and the pujas at the temple," Anand's father argued.

"But he must learn more than that if he's going to become a great pundit and fulfill his karma," urged Anand's uncle.

"Let him come with us to Bombay. We'll see that he faithfully fulfills all his priestly duties. In fact, he can serve as our household priest. But we'll also send him to the finest schools where he can prepare himself for the university. You shouldn't deny him the same privileges your father gave you."

And so at last Anand's parents reluctantly agreed to allow him to go to Bombay with his aunt and uncle, in essence to become their son—and their priest.

Anand recalls the parting with his mother, to whom he was very close. Indian mothers have a special attachment to their sons, for they remain in the home, while daughters leave once they are married. Girls are frequently reminded, "This isn't your home. You're going to be the daughter in another home." So there is a tendency for mothers to feel closer to their sons.

Luxmi seemed to have a premonition that Anand would never return home to live again, for as she held him close she urged, "Remember what we've taught you, Anand. Always be truthful and kind; keep your word and be faithful to our gods."

Anand clung to his mother, for now that the moment of parting had come, some of the excitement of the journey faded. His cousins had painted a rosy picture of Bombay, with its trams and buses, and the school where he would be attending with other boys his age.

But somehow the separation from his parents and his little sister hadn't seemed real until this moment. He looked around the familiar temple compound: the red-tiled mud and stone house that was the only home he'd ever known, the ancient temple with its imposing columns and colorful gods, the coconut trees waving in the breeze, the beauty and peace of the countryside.

Then suddenly the bus arrived, and confusion reigned as luggage was stored and his aunt corralled the four little girls to say their good-byes and climb aboard. Anand felt strange in his city clothes, for his aunt said he could not arrive in Bombay in a dhoti. He huddled down on the bench next to his uncle, wishing with all his heart that he was still standing by the roadside with his parents waving good-bye to his uncle and aunt, instead of sitting here disappearing into the distance.

Thus in 1942, the twelve-year-old "priest-in-training" arrived in Bombay, the gateway to India. He was no doubt unaware of the political tensions swirling through the city at that time.

Mahatma Gandhi had been imprisoned once again by the British for his call to the All-India Congress Committee that the British "quit India." The cry for independence, to which the Congress party had sworn for the first time in 1930, the year of Anand's birth, was steadily growing stronger and more urgent.

But when the train pulled into the famed Victoria Station bringing Anand to his new home, India's freedom was the least of his concerns.

Everything was bewildering and frightening as he scurried after his relatives. The coaches seemed to stretch for miles down the track, and he had to hurry to keep up with the barefooted porters who carried their valises and boxes stacked on their heads as they darted through the crowds. Anand was afraid he would get lost in the crush of the crowd. He had never seen so many people in one place before.

Quickly the porters disappeared up the stairs leading to an overpass across the tracks, and he scurried after them, pushing past carts loaded with aromatic spiced foods and succulent fruits. He almost ran into a boy selling tea in disposable clay cups from window to window of a heavily loaded train ready to leave.

Anand had to be careful not to trip over bundles and boxes piled indiscriminantly on the concourse. What looked like a pile of rags turned out to be a man with a dirty cloth pulled up over his face as he slept, undisturbed by the sounds and smells around him.

Without warning a loud screech of steam filled the air, and just beside Anand, so close he could touch them, wheels ground into motion. Fascinated, he turned to watch the train chug forward, slowly at first, increasing speed as the white steam rose into the blackened girders which supported the roof of the station. For a moment Anand lost sight of the wicker case on the porter's head who had been his guide. Frightened, Anand feared he was lost.

But just then he felt a hand grab his arm, and he welcomed the sight of his aunt's worried face. She realized how easily a child could be lost in this mass of humanity, especially a village boy who had never seen the sights of the big city before, and made sure she had a hand on him until they reached the exit.

Anand would never forget the ride from Victoria Station to his aunt and uncle's home. No one in the village of Dhargal owned a car. Now and again Anand had seen a truck pass by on the main road, and the weekly bus stopped to pick up passengers. But here Bombay's streets were crowded, not only with cars, but bicycles, Victorian buggies drawn by prancing horses, and carts pulled by oxen. The noise of horns and bells and whistles was deafening to his ears, accustomed only to the temple gong and the pigeons cooing in the rafters.

Every time the driver blew his horn to pass another car, Anand was sure they would have an accident. "How do they all keep from hitting each other?" he wondered. And his cousins laughed as Anand threw his arm over his face to protect himself.

But the greatest wonder of all was that this car they were riding in was his uncle's, and the chauffeur who drove it worked for him. The wealth of his new family began to sink in as they entered Marine Drive where the homes were almost as big as the temple in Dhargal. Up and up they drove into Malabar Hill. As they turned a corner, Anand caught his breath. The sea spread before him in all its shimmering iridescence.

Then the car stopped before heavy gates which were opened by a watchman, and they drove into the beautiful grounds of his uncle's villa.

For the first few days, Anand had difficulty finding his way around the "bungalow," as his uncle called it. Anand's own room looked out upon the sea—an ever-changing sight he never wearied of. A trail led down through thick undergrowth to the beach below. In the years ahead, Anand would often go to a sheltered spot on that beach for meditation.

As the opening of school at the beginning of June drew closer, Anand's heart was filled with fear and dread. He'd never attended school in his life—his father and the other priests had been his only teachers. His uncle had used his considerable influence through his job in the government service to get Anand into one of the best English medium schools in the city.

Though he was well qualified to enter seventh grade with his own age group, Anand had to start in the fifth grade because he had never learned English.

Studies were no problem, for Anand had a keen mind; but the interaction with the other boys was more difficult. He couldn't understand how they could laugh and make noise when the teacher was talking. If he had done that to his father, he would have been severely punished.

He looked forward eagerly to letters from home; both his father and mother wrote once or twice a month. His father always admonished, "Keep yourself in the same traditions. Don't forget the promise I have made to god about you." Anand knew that his father fully expected him to return to Dhargal to teach Hinduism at the temple.

Each year during the school holidays, Anand returned home for three to four weeks. His father would grill him about his Hindu practices, and test his knowledge of scripture and his memorization of the mantras. He was pleased at Anand's report of how he performed the daily pujas in his uncle's shrine, as well as in the family altar. It was a time when father and son could talk over the various rituals so that Anand could improve his service to his uncle's family.

But by now the life in the city had become such a part of him that Anand found it easy to leave home when the holidays were over. He missed the excitement of Bombay in the slow and easy pace of the temple compound.

And the excitement in Bombay was heating up, for the city was a hotbed of political intrigue, processions and petitions. In 1946, after Gandhi was again released from prison, Anand attended a mass rally and heard the legendary leader in person. Though Anand was too busy with his studies to become embroiled in political movements, he followed the news with keen interest.

As a government servant, his uncle maintained strict neutrality on the surface, but as they discussed the issues over the evening meal, it was clear that he, too, was eager for independence from the British.

The night of India's freedom in January 1947 was a time of riotous celebration. Crowds all over Bombay went wild with joy. Everywhere people gathered around radios in public places. Anand and his uncle's family had a radio at home and listened to the ceremonies as the fateful hour of midnight struck.

After midnight the city was aglow with lights, and the family took a drive to see the displays and fireworks. Thousands swarmed into the Taj Mahal Hotel, the site of imperial elegance to which they had been denied entrance, to taste of their newfound freedom.

In 1950 Anand began to attend Bombay University. He continued his interest in religion and philosophy, and began his bachelor's honors degree in philosophy. Bombay University was a cauldron of Communist unrest during these early days of independence, and there were dozens of cell groups meeting.

Always a loner, Anand spent a great deal of his spare time reading. His honors program consisted of sixteen subjects, including Western Philosophy. He studied the writings of Lenin, Hegel, and Marx as part of his courses, and soon found himself drawn to their progressive teachings.

During the early days after independence, the influence of Communism was rampant on the university campus. Ever interested in new philosophies, Anand began attending a Communist cell group regularly. Soon the students recognized his astute ability to interpret and teach, and he found himself guiding discussions and clarifying points of Communist principles to other students.

One of Anand's assignments was to run classes for the laboring people in the slum areas of Bombay. He would distill the economic theories from his vast reading into simple and practical gut issues: "Why are you poor? Compare what you're earning to what the owner is earning! You don't have to put up with this inequality."

For the first time in his life, Anand walked among the grinding poverty that cursed so many millions of Indians. He watched children squatting to relieve themselves in open sewers, while a few feet farther along a woman washed her clothes in the filthy stream.

He walked through the muddy alleyways, turned into fetid quagmires by the monsoons. He watched rats nibble at the toes of children sleeping on gunny sacks on the muddy ground.

Anand's eyes were opened to hunger and disease and hopelessness. "I visited where the laborers lived," he recalls. "I saw their squalid conditions, fifteen or sixteen people living in a one-room shack. There was no running water, no sanitation facilities. The people who had jobs worked like animals for a few cents a day."

He couldn't help compare their lot with his gracious lifestyle up on Malabar Hill.

And as he devoured Communist literature and its interpretation of history, he became more and more disturbed at Hinduism's lack of explanation for why things were as they were.

It perturbed him that there was no written Indian history before the sixth or seventh century A. D. It seemed incredible to him that Hindus saw no value in history because of their fatalistic acceptance that all that occurs in this life is a direct result of past incarnations. Nothing can be changed.

"Hinduism always looks back," Anand explains today. "All you have in this life is a result of fulfilling your karma—whatever you have done in your past life. And whatever you are doing now will determine your next birth. The Harijan (outcaste) does what he is expected to do, and the Brahmin does whatever is predestined for him."

But Anand began to realize that Hinduism had been used to safeguard the high caste or rich people. As he studied recent Indian history, it was evident that the Brahmins had supported the kings against the poor people.

Slowly Anand admitted to himself that Hinduism, with its fatalistic teaching and resignation to personal karma, would never solve the desperate problems of poverty and injustice in India which he saw all around him and which affected him more acutely as he grew older.

For the first time, Anand did not go home for the school holidays in the summer of 1950. He was too busy with his Communist activities. He tried to explain this to his mother, but from her letters he could tell she was hurt.

His earlier training in journalism now came in handy. He was asked to write numerous articles for the student newspaper. Secretly he hoped to make a career of journalism, though he knew his father would never approve.

For Anand, the teachings of Marx and Lenin were logical and intellectual. Yet while the poverty of the masses and the inequities of the Indian system perturbed him, he had no difficulty accepting the good life of his foster home.

As the pampered adopted son of an influential and wealthy Brahmin family, Anand lacked nothing. There were always plenty of servants to care for his slightest whim; a chauffeured car waiting for his requests. As the family's personal priest, he fulfilled his obligations meticulously and unstintingly. He was respected in the community and often called upon to offer special pujas, to officiate at weddings and cremations, and to appease the gods in times of trouble.

Anand was a private person—his years of seclusion and intense study enabled him to get along without intimate friendships; he felt self-fulfilled. His books, his position as Brahmin priest, and the security of ritual and ceremony gave his life direction and meaning. He had never questioned his Hindu faith, rooted so deeply in his subconscious.

But now as he read the disturbing philosophies of the dialectic materialists, the squalid poverty which he saw on every hand began to take on new meaning. The inequities of a social system that relegated 20 percent of the population to the destitute untouchable class, with no hope for change in this life, began to trouble him.

What was the purpose of their endless sacrifices and daily rituals? The gods simply locked them into their wretchedness, to live their miserable existence without complaint—to suffer pain to its numbness, to give something out of their nothing, to appease the gods' anger so that perchance they would return in the next life as a man rather than a woman? Or a farmer rather than a barber?

No wonder the promise of freedom and a classless society began to intrigue Anand's compassionate heart—hidden in his objective and disciplined mind.

Finally after months of agonizing struggle and debate, Anand had to admit, "Hinduism had no answer for India's problems, and no assurance for my future personally. My faith was not strong enough to withstand the arguments of Communism. What really attracted me was a very intellectual and logical philosophy."

By now Anand could pinpoint the weaknesses of Hindu philosophy. He recalls his utter despair with its fatalism. "Everything is dependent upon what you have done in the past. And whatever you are doing now will follow you in your next birth."

Even after his final repudiation of Hinduism, Anand continued to practice his rituals faithfully, though empty and void of meaning. Yet, he was still a Hindu. He could explain this dichotomy only by saying, "By being a Communist, a person does not cease to be a Hindu; he is still a Hindu, and he will die a Hindu."

Thus, when he told his aunt and uncle about his Communist activities, they listened with interest. Perhaps they were unaware of how completely he had renounced his belief in the gods and reincarnation. As long as he faithfully maintained his ablutions, priestly role and Brahmin behavior, that was enough to satisfy them. They knew others in the caste community who'd taken this route before him.

And other great Hindus had followed the same path. Jawaharlal Nehru, the first prime minister of India, was an avowed atheist and a sympathetic Communist. Yet when his fatal heart attack struck, he was heard to call out, "Oh god, save me." His deep religious roots were still there.

But Anand's sense of satisfaction and confidence was not long-lived. As he continued reading and studying, he was exposed to literature by ex-communists. He read *The God that Failed*, edited by Arthur Koesler, which explained why different people left the Communist Party. Another influential book, *Managerial Revolution,* by James Burnham, exposed the failure of Marxism in Russia.

In predicting the failure of both capitalism and socialism, Burnham painted a scathing denunciation of the very principles Anand expected would bring hope to his tortured land.

Rather than a classless society, Burnham exposed the "workers state" as a myth in which the workers were heavily exploited; the idea of a perfectly free and equal utopia as an illusion.

Dismayed, Anand read Burnham's indictment, "The workers . . . sensed that the freedom and end of privilege which they had thought the revolution was to bring, were giving way to a new form of class rule."[1]

His dreams for an India healed of class and caste distinctions by the surgery of revolution were shattered as Anand read Burnham's revelation of life in Russia in the 1930s:

"There has been not the slightest tendency toward the free, classless society of socialism as socialism was defined in the prior expectations. There is no democracy in Russia. There is no control, social or economic or political, exercised by the masses. . . . There is . . . not merely graft and corruption but systematic class exploitation on the basis of the state-owned economy."[2]

But more than his reading, Anand was disturbed by what he saw as the lack of moral consistency in the party leaders. "I began to realize that in the Communist strategy a person is expected to kill even his own brother if he is going against authority or party politics. Party was everything to a Communist—not relationships, not honesty. The end justified the means."

This moral deficiency troubled Anand, who had been brought up in a home where the importance of family relationships and moral character were deeply ingrained.

For a period of about six months, Anand tried to resolve the disillusionments and inconsistencies he saw in Communism. There was no question about returning to the Hindu faith; once demolished, it was gone forever. But he craved a philosophy that could not be shattered by careful scrutiny or intense exposure. It was as though his heart and mind were starving and he tried to hang on to any shreds of truth that would keep him from total inner emptiness.

"My whole upbringing was that mentally I needed to have some faith to live for," he confesses, "but I found nothing." Late in 1953, in the midst of this turmoil, Anand was asked to participate in a debate, which was part of a great peace movement all over the world organized by Communist students. The subject which was to be debated before several thousand students was: "Will there be peace in this world?"

Anand accepted the honor, but even as he prepared, he knew he had no answers. Would he make a fool of himself?

---

[1] Burnham, James, *The Managerial Revolution,* Indiana University Press, Bloomington, Indiana, 1941, p. 214.
[2] Ibid, page 220.

6

The Sacred Cord Removed

"With control in the hands of the masses, and power out of the hands of the bourgeoisie, then and only then will there be permanent peace on the earth."

Anand sat down to polite applause from the thousand or more students who had crowded into the university hall to hear the debate, "Will there be peace on the earth?"

He had been asked to represent Bombay University as the one who could best expound the Communist philosophy—but his words had the hollowness of an empty drum. Anand knew he'd let his fellow students down, and his face burned with embarrassment as he took his seat.

His arguments had been weak. How could he convince his audience, when he could not convince himself? Peace on earth? His own nation had just come through a bloody and cruel civil war after the Partition in 1947, and the hatreds between Hindu and Muslim were never far beneath the surface.

He barely heard the opposing side's response, so overwhelmed was he by his own failure, and worse, his own confusion. After years of study, all he'd managed to discover was that no ideology could stand the test of scrutiny.

Burnham's words, from a book he'd read recently, flashed across the screen of Anand's mind: "The power of an ideology has several dimensions—it is shown both by the number of men that it sways and also by the extent to which it sways them; that is, whether they are moved only to verbal protestations of loyalty, or to a will to sacrifice and die under its slogans."[1]

So far, Anand had found nothing to die for—and little to live for. Lost in his depressed confusion, he hardly heard the opposing team present their arguments. One of the debaters, Joseph, was a fellow student from Goa. He was a Goanese, half Portuguese rather than a pure Indian, and Anand had never spoken with him.

But as Joseph drew his arguments to a conclusion, Anand's mind was suddenly jerked out of its reverie as he heard him say, "According to my faith, peace will come in this world only when Jesus Christ comes back to establish His kingdom on earth—and not until then."

There was little applause when he finished. The Hindu Communist audience wanted to hear nothing about a Western god.

Anand paid little attention to the closing arguments, and hardly cared who won or lost. He slipped out of the hall, almost in a daze. His disenchantment with socialism was now as total as with Hinduism. And as he drove through the streets of Bombay towards home, he ached for his suffering, hopeless people—and for himself.

Yet gnawing at his mind in the days after the debate was Joseph's statement, "Peace will come in this world only when Jesus Christ returns to establish his kingdom on this earth."

Jesus Christ? Anand recalled how disgusted his parents had been about his followers in Goa. They would return from a visit to the capital, Panjim, with revolting stories of drinking and debauchery by those who called themselves Christians. When he was small they wouldn't even talk about the loose moral behaviour between men and women, who pawed each other in public, demonstrating physical contact that no respectable Hindu man and wife would allow to be seen even in their own home.

Jesus Christ? What could that Western god have to do with peace on earth, with solutions to the pain and poverty of India?

But why would Joseph have spoken so openly about it in front of that mass of students? Didn't he know they would ridicule and laugh at him? What kind of courage did he have to take such a risk? Once again Anand recalled Burnham's definition of a powerful ideology— one for whom men would be willing to sacrifice and die.

In later years Anand would describe those days following the debate: "I tried to forget what I had heard, but I couldn't. That name seemed to be hooked into my mind, and could not be shaken loose.

"Then it struck me. I had studied just about everything else, why not see what this was all about? So about ten days after the debate I contacted Joseph to find out where I could read more about Jesus."

Joseph was a Roman Catholic who somehow had discovered the power of Scripture, long before Vatican II. When Anand approached him rather apprehensively about his statement at the debate, he passed off his interest as a desire to investigate yet another philosophy. Joseph promised to bring him a book the next day.

When they met again, Joseph handed Anand a small booklet. "Read this Gospel of Matthew. It will give you the story of Jesus Christ."

Anand took the tiny book, hardly bigger than a pamphlet, wondering how a philosophy worth studying could be contained in so few pages. His first readings were disappointing: "As of the geneology of Jesus Christ the son of David, the son of Abraham," it began. "Abraham was the father of Isaac, Isaac the father of Jacob, Jacob the father of Judah and his brothers."

The story of the birth of Jesus reminded Anand of some of the Hindu myths he'd heard all his life. The story of Joseph's escape into Egypt to save the baby Jesus' life, and Herod's murder of boy babies, because he feared for his throne, was reminiscent of Krishna's escape from Kamsa.

Anand's Communist-trained mind rejected these stories as it had the Hindu myths. Disappointed, he put the booklet aside and returned to his other studies.

Yet, there was something that haunted him. Was it Joseph's courage in the face of ridicule? Or a power he could not explain that kept bringing the name of Jesus Christ into his consciousness? Should he give this philosophy another chance, and read further to expose himself to its broader teaching?

One day Anand made a point of seeking Joseph out at the university. "What is there about Jesus Christ that would make you claim he'll bring peace to the earth?" Anand questioned. "I just don't see there's anything better here than Hinduism has to offer."

Joseph was evidently not a well-taught Christian, though in retrospect Anand is sure he was born again. All he could tell Anand was, "Read on—read the Gospels. God will talk to you and show you the truth."

With that advice, Anand decided to try once again. One evening he settled down in his room with the Christian Gospels—Joseph had given him three more by this time—and determined he would read them through.

As he began reading the teachings of Jesus a strange reaction took hold of him. He who had always been so unemotional and analytical, found his heart awakened and touched; an unfamiliar and totally uncomfortable response for one who had learned to submerge every-thing into nothingness.

"Blessed are the meek," he read, "for they will inherit the earth."

The outcaste, the poor, and the masses were promised hope in this ideology.

His eyes wanted to race across the pages and absorb it all in one movement, as Anand was swept on by the magnificent story.

But his heart could not hurry.

"You have heard that it was said, 'eye for eye, and tooth for tooth.' But I tell you, Do not resist an evil person. If someone strikes you on the right cheek, turn to him the other also."

Anand closed his eyes and could see in contrast the mother god-dess, Kali, bedecked with a chain of human skulls, and blood running from her mouth from those she devoured in her anger.

Night after night he read, slowly, savoring each thought that flashed with new insights across his mind, which had never worked in harness with his heart before.

During this time Anand was asked to review the film, *The Robe*, for a local newspaper. It was a moving, enthralling story of people in classical Rome who had been captivated by Jesus, the One who had worn the robe which retained its power even after He died. It brought to life the One he'd been reading about in Matthew. Its high moral tone, so different from the usual Indian films he'd seen, made a tremendous impact on him. Anand also read *The Robe*, which was well-written and entertaining. Could this be the same Jesus Christ that Joseph was expecting to return to earth to establish a kingdom?

In the weeks ahead Anand returned again and again to the Chris-tian scriptures—drawn by the moral purity and perfection of Christ, yet looking for the flaws that must be there. Nothing else had been able to stand up to his scrutiny.

He describes this period of searching in his printed testimony, *I Was a Shastri*, "I read through Matthew and the other Gospels. Much that I read I did not understand, but I was like a parched desert, soaking up the life-giving water."

As the full force of Christ's purity and perfection emerged from his reading, a strange and repugnant emotion poured over Anand—the deep sense of guilt for his own sinfulness.

"I never felt myself as a guilty sinner before," he confesses. "According to Hindu philosophy I was completely all right."

After all, his karma from his previous life had put him in a high Brahmin home, given him an excellent mind and body, placed him in a wealthy foster home with all the material things he could want. He must have lived a life that pleased the gods.

He had prestige and power; he was respected as a Hindu priest and teacher. The idea of being a "sinner" was repulsive to him.

But now as he read of Christ's love, His unselfishness, tender compassion to the weak and helpless, His constant concern for others without thought for His own comfort, Anand could find no fault. And his own life, mirrored before that perfect One, was flawed and sinful.

He could not help but compare Jesus to the gods that he had known; they helped only the ones doing right, and destroyed those who did wrong.

Anand especially recalled the story of Shiva, one of the triumverate of Hindu divinities who was known as the destroyer. Shiva had killed his own son, Ganesha, in a fit of jealousy. Remorseful, he sought another head for the decapitated body, and took the first thing he could find, an elephant head. The elephant-head god is one of the most popular of the lesser gods, the patron deity of students and teachers. Everywhere Anand turned the contrast between the moral perfection of Christ and the imperfection of the Hindu gods, or the Communist philosophy, became apparent.

And yet the search for truth was not easy. How did he know Jesus was real, and not just another god, granted, of higher moral character? He'd spent years studying the Hindu scriptures—now here was another book that claimed authenticity. Where did it fit into truth?

Anand recalled that other great Hindus had been fascinated by the personality, life, and teachings of Jesus. The nineteenth century guru, Ramakrishna, had seen a vision of Jesus as he concentrated on a painting of Him. Jesus became an incarnation of love. Ramakrishna claimed that Jesus had appeared to him, "The son of Man kissed the Son of the Divine Mother [Kali] and was dissolved in her."[2]

The guru realized his identity with all gods—Kali, Rama, Hanuman, Jesus, etc. He came to the conclusion that Christianity, too, was a road that led to the awareness of God.

But the more Anand read the Gospels, the more convinced he became that Christianity claimed there was no other way to the true

God—that he could not coat his Hindu foundation and Communist superstructure with a covering of Christianity.

If only he could talk with someone who could guide his thinking. He found Joseph of little help. He had a simple faith, but the more Anand talked with him, the more he found his Catholic traditions had little intellectual basis for him, and his knowledge of the Scriptures was limited. Joseph could not understand why Anand had so many "intellectual questions." When he could not answer, he simply encouraged, "You must just have faith, that's all."

There were several other Catholic students at the university, but Anand didn't know them, or whether or not they were more versed in their religion than Joseph. Besides Joseph, he knew no other Christian.

After almost four months of tension and struggle, Anand was desperate for an answer. He knew he could not continue vacillating; yet the consequences of his accepting Christianity as truth would be devastating.

He wished he could talk this over with his father, who had always been an open and honest seeker for truth. But he had to find the answer for himself. Is Christ really God? Or is He just another mythological figure like those he'd been worshipping all his life?

Finally one evening, the 23rd of January 1954, Anand made his way to his favorite spot by the sea, determined to settle the matter. "I felt I could not go on like this any longer," he recalls. "If there was a God—and by that time that meant Jesus Christ—I had to have Him make it quite plain to me."

Even after his ideological break with Hinduism, Anand found great comfort in concentrated meditation and controlled breathing, focusing his thoughts, and relaxing his body. He could sit motionless in a position of meditation, cross-legged, straight-backed, for hours—and find the experience refreshing.

As he meditated by the shore that evening, the blazing sun burned a luminescent path across the waters, turning them to shimmering gold and silver. He hardly saw the children playing on the sands, or the hawkers calling their wares. It was his moment of truth. Oblivious of passersby, he slipped forward on his knees and brought his palms together towards his forehead in an attitude of worship. But his prayer was one he'd never prayed before. He found himself talking heart to heart: "Jesus . . . Jesus if You are alive, I want to know definitely at this time. I would like to have the experience of my sins forgiven. Give me the assurance that You are a living God, not just something 'up there.'"

Anand involuntarily lifted his head and looked heavenward. "Give me the experience of your presence—a definite experience." Tears began streaming down his cheeks in an emotion he'd never felt before. "And if you do that, I promise that I will give my life to You."

Even to this day it's very difficult for Anand to describe what happened. "Somehow I felt the real presence of Christ there. Someone holy just touched me and surrounded me. I will never forget that experience. I felt such a peace in my heart that everything else was gone. I felt free and utter joy. All my questions were gone. All the turmoil was gone—the conflict, everything—just a serene peace, calm and quietness.

"I really felt that if I could reach out my hand I could touch Him. His presence was so real.

"And that's what changed my life—nothing else. I was really committed to Christ . . . and from that moment I was willing to face anything because of that experience. I wanted to tell everyone I met what had happened to me."

But there was one more thing he had to do before he left the seashore. Slowly Anand unbuttoned his shirt, and gingerly touched the sacred cord which he'd worn since the priest had placed it across his shoulders.

Then with one determined effort, he jerked it from his body and flung it far into the sea. For a moment he watched it bob in the crest of a wave, and then disappear into the darkening waters. There was no turning back now.

Throwing the sacred cord into the sea was a total and complete break with the past. Later Anand explained, "I knew I didn't need it anymore."

In the next two months, Anand's very sanity would be threatened by excruciating emotional pain. Only this life-changing experience on the shores of the Indian Ocean would serve as his rudder.

---

[1]Burnham, James, *The Managerial Revolution,* Indiana University Press, Bloomington, Indiana, 1941, p. 56.

[2]Lemaitre, Solange, *Ramakrishna and the Vitality of Hinduism,* Funk and Wagnalls, New York, 1969, p. 110.

7

A Father's Heart Broken

Anand found his uncle at the dinner table when he returned from the seashore. Though he was too excited to eat, Anand joined him and began describing his earthshaking experience.

"I've had a vision of God, Uncle. He surrounded me with His presence so that I could almost touch Him. My heart is so full of peace."

At first his uncle was interested and wanted to know more. After all, few priests had this experience, though they sought it all their lives. But as he questioned Anand more, his pleasure turned to dismay.

"Why would you seek an experience with the Christian God, Anand? We have our own gods whom you've worshipped all your life. What has He ever done for you?"

No matter how Anand tried to explain, it simply did not make sense to his uncle, who denounced the whole experience as foolishness.

"You'll soon get over it; all your studies are going to your head."

But Anand continued to try to tell him of Jesus and the Gospels he'd been reading. Then his uncle became angry.

"You're a Hindu, Anand. Christianity is for Westerners, but it will never be accepted here in India. You're a Brahmin priest, with years of training behind you. Now you're finally ready to fulfill your father's plans for you. You'd break his heart if he learned of this."

The two men parted that evening, the matter lying unresolved between them. In the weeks ahead, Anand continued to perform pujas for his aunt and uncle, but he became more and more uncomfortable about it. He tried to explain to them that they had no meaning for him any more.

"I have a new God now to whom I can pray anytime without idols or rituals. He is so close to me I can almost touch Him. His presence that I felt that night is still there."

But his relatives were adamant. "You don't do it for yourself, you do it for us because we believe in the gods. You are just the medium. You do it for our merit, not yours."

Meanwhile, at school Anand sought out Joseph whenever he could. They would stop for coffee, or sit on the university lawn, while Anand plied him with questions about the Gospels.

Anand tried to put the depth of his experience by the shore into words, but the years of disciplined self-control and impassive responses were not easily thawed.

Yet Joseph seemed to understand what had happened and did his best to answer the questions Anand kept asking. Anand knew Jesus was the divine Son of the one true God—but how this all fell together into a plan for life and beyond was still a mystery to him.

Joseph never once invited Anand to attend his church with him. Perhaps he realized that Anand would become more confused seeing images that resembled the gods he'd worshipped for so long. But the two young men forged an inexplicable bond as they discussed the Bible and analyzed its meaning.

Then one day Anand noticed that Joseph was missing from the lecture hall. At first he wasn't concerned because students often missed classes. But two weeks passed, and then three, and Joseph did not return, nor did Anand see him around the campus. By now Anand was sure that he was ill, or had returned home for some family emergency, but no one seemed to know anything about him.

It was almost four weeks since he'd last seen Joseph before Anand ran into one of his Goanese friends who told him the shocking news. Joseph had fallen ill with typhoid and in just a few days had died.

Joseph's death struck a painful and bewildering blow. Anand knew no other Christian; there was no one else to talk with or of whom to ask questions. He was left now with only the Gospels, which he continued to pour over with a burning fervor.

Then Anand received the exciting news that his parents would be coming to Bombay. They were on their way to the sacred bathing festival in Allahabad. He hadn't seen his parents in four years, and he suddenly realized how much he had missed them.

But now he had a special reason for wanting to see his father. He was anxious to share his experience with him. He knew that the Shastri had tried all his life to receive such a vision as he'd had. Anand's father had studied different philosophies of Hinduism, and was always willing to listen to new teaching.

But his father had been frustrated because he'd not been able to have the experience which many of the old monks wrote about. They described in detail their visions of god as they meditated in the jungles.

"I felt that if my father could understand my vision, he would also accept what I had accepted," Anand sadly recalls. "At that time it was not a question of changing religion. I was just thinking subjectively about a living, true experience. I wasn't thinking at that time about joining institutional Christianity. So, I felt my father might seek the same experience. I was eager to explain so he wouldn't misunderstand what had happened to me."

As the days drew closer to his parents' arrival, a disquieting uneasiness filled Anand's heart. He knew how his father felt about Christianity. Would he have the ability to answer his questions and disarm his arguments? He was not afraid for his own faith. If anything, it had grown since Joseph's tragic death, and he was more sure than ever that he had found real truth.

And then the day arrived. His parents hadn't changed much in the four years since he'd last been home. His mother's brown eyes sparkled with love as he folded her in his arms.

And he could hardly believe what he saw when he greeted Pushbanjali. Why, she'd become a beautiful young lady. "How old are you now, Pushba?" he'd asked.

And she'd smiled shyly at this grown-up brother of hers and responded softly, "Almost fourteen."

His father looked well and strong. Anand fell on his knees and touched his feet in the traditional greeting of a young man to an elder. Though his father said little, Anand could sense that he was proud of his son, so successful at the university, so accomplished in languages, well trained in his priestly duties and respected in the community.

With a sense of trepidation, Anand joined the men as they gathered around the Western style dinner table, laden with aromatic curries, salads, and steaming vegetables. His married cousins and their husbands and children lived nearby, so they were quite a crowd. The servants had been busy preparing food since the early hours of the morning. While the men enjoyed their meal in a jovial spirit of reunion, he could hear the women chattering and laughing as they exchanged confidences in the next room.

But he knew that these happy moments of togetherness and eager sharing of family stories would soon be disturbed. His uncle had made it very clear that he would reveal Anand's dangerous dereliction at the first opportunity.

"Your father only has two days here in Bombay, and he'll want to have as much time as possible to get these heretical ideas out of your head," he'd warned.

And so it was that as soon as the servants had cleared the table, Anand's uncle looked meaningfully at him and then spoke up. "Anna, we have a serious matter to discuss. It has to do with your son."

A startled look came across Anand's father's usually impassive face. He could almost see him begin to frame a question like," Has he become an atheist?"

Without trying to soften the blow, Anand's uncle announced, "Anand is becoming involved with Christianity."

Then Anand broke in, "Let me explain, Uncle. This is something I should tell Father myself."

Anand could hardly bear to look at his father's ashen face. "I've had a vision, Father—a vision of God. He was so real to me that I felt I could touch Him."

"A vision of god? Impossible," his father retorted. "The ancient monks spent many years in meditation to gain this experience. I have never had it, though I've sought it all my life. How could you, a mere boy, have such an experience?"

"But it's true, Father. I've been seeking truth for a long time. I even joined the Communists at the university for a time—but they have no morality. Then I began studying the Christian Scriptures—and there I found a new, holy God—Jesus Christ."

Anand's voice faltered. For as long as he could remember he had revered and respected his father—not only as father, but as his priest and pundit. His heart broke as he saw the pain and disbelief in his face. He hung his head.

The Shastri continued to stare in silence and disbelief. And then for the first time in his life, Anand saw his father lose his temper. The Shastri was unable to control the rage that burned within him at the thought of his only son becoming a despised Christian.

"You must be losing your mind," he shouted.

Then he jumped to his feet and pointed an accusing finger at his brother-in-law. "I was afraid of this years ago when you wanted to take the boy to Bombay. I knew he would be tainted by the loose morality and contaminated life-styles of this city. I was right; he should never have come here to live with you."

As their voices raised in anger the two brothers-in-law would have come to blows, but Anand interfered.

"No Father, don't blame Uncle. He's been scolding me for this ever since he heard about it the first time."

But Anand's father struck the table with his fist and would not listen to his son. "I don't want to hear any more of this nonsense. The pundits and gurus have been studying the scriptures of Hinduism long before Christianity was born. Do you think you know more than they?"

There was little sleep for Anand that night—or for anyone in the house, for that matter. Anand could hear the murmur of voices from his parents' room into the early hours of the morning. He spent much of the night in prayer, seeking comfort from the One who had become everything to him.

"Lord Jesus, help me to explain about You so my parents will understand, and believe. Lord, my father is so hurt—I have never seen him this angry before. He dedicated me to his god when my brothers died, and now I'm making him break that promise. Somehow reach his heart and show him that what I'm doing is right. Help me to be able to explain the beauty and purity of Jesus to him, so he will also be able to believe. Help him to understand so that he can also have this experience with You."

With those entreaties Anand fell asleep, hoping that he would have another opportunity the next day to discuss this with his father before he left for Allahabad.

In the strained atmosphere of the household the next morning, Anand found no time to talk with his father. Anand saw the Shastri sitting motionless in a position of meditation before the household shrine for hours, and he did not dare interrupt.

But he sought out his mother as she was repacking their things for the long trip to Allahabad by train that night.

He could tell from her reddened eyes that she had been crying, but she smiled invitingly at Anand and gestured for him to sit down.

He dropped down on the floor beside her, as he had so often in the years past when he was a boy growing up in Goa.

She began talking as she continued folding clothes, and her words became indelibly imprinted in his mind.

"I don't understand everything your father has been telling me about your experience with the Christian God, Anand. It doesn't make sense to me. But I trust you, and if you have really had this vision that you're talking about, then follow it. See if it's real."

Her voice dropped, and she continued with a touch of fear. "I don't know if you're going to be able to stay in this house now, Anand. Your aunt and uncle are very upset about your talk about Jesus."

Anand had already faced up to the possibility that he would have to leave his comfortable home and his adopted family, though nothing had been said to him yet. No doubt they were giving him time to change his mind.

But his mother added, "I want you to promise me two things Anand."

He nodded his head and responded softly, "If I can, I will, Mother."

"Never spread your hand to beg from strangers for your support. If this experience is real, then you must live by faith and your God will provide whatever you need.

"And as far as women go Anand—don't behave in such a way that you will bring disgrace on your family. Respect women—not as things. Live a pure life—not like the Christians in Goa that have disgusted me all my life. You're not going to become like one of them, are you Anand?"

"No, Mother, I've always tried to live a pure life as you and Father taught me. But now I have a pure and holy God who has given me His example to follow, and His Spirit to help me. I've never had such perfection to pattern my life after in the Hindu gods. I promise that you won't have to be ashamed of me."

His mother smiled and patted his shoulder. "I'm not sure what the future is going to be like for us, Anand. Your father may not allow you to come back to the temple in Goa again, unless you give up this new faith. But I know you'll keep your promises to me, and I'll pray to Lord Vishnu for you."

Suddenly it was time to leave for the train station. Relatives who were traveling with Anand's parents arrived. Last-minute provisions were gathered because the family would be camping out on the river bank during the several days of the festival. As everything was being loaded into the car, Anand tried one last time to break his father's silence.

"Father—we should have talked more."

"When I come back we'll talk again," his father responded, looking coldly into Anand's eyes. "You can tell me about your experience with the Christian God. If you can prove to me that what you've experienced is true, then I'll seek to find Him, too.

"But if you can't, then I expect you to go through the ritual cleansing and continue preparing for the priesthood."

Anand watched the car until it turned the corner, heading for the railway station where his relatives would catch the train for the great Kumbh Mela festival in Allahabad. Long after the car was out of sight, Anand stood there pondering his father's last words. And he would ponder their meaning for the rest of his life.

8
Death at the Ganges

The early weeks of 1954 passed slowly for Anand. A strained atmosphere prevailed in his uncle's house. Anand continued performing pujas for the household, though it became more and more distasteful to him.

It was as though his future hinged on his father's return from the Kumbh Mela. His aunt and uncle believed that the Shastri would bring his wayward son to his senses.

Anand continued to find strength as he read the Gospels over and over. Many of the beautiful passages sank into his memory, as the Hindu scriptures had in the past. For a long time he'd been unaware that his near-perfect photographic memory was not simply the normal outcome of a disciplined mind. He just knew that he could recall almost anything he'd read as though it were printed on a mental page in his mind.

On February 4 his uncle brought a small item in the daily newspaper to his attention. There had evidently been some problems at the Kumbh Mela and several people had been hurt in the crush of the crowd.

"Something like that happens every year. It can hardly be helped when almost a million people crowd into one open space," his uncle had commented.

But the Kumbh Mela in 1954 was an unusually auspicious festival, and an estimated five million gathered on the shores of the Ganges to bathe in the holy waters. Each year pundits and astrologers determined the most propitious moment to enter the water, according to the phases of the moon, and the alignment of the sun, moon, and the planet Jupiter. The Mela is held each year at the winter solstice, but every twelve years is a Kumbh Mela which is particularly holy.

In 1954, however, for reasons understood only by the Hindu astrologers and pundits, a series of conditions had come together which occurred only once in 144 years. Therefore, it was considered one thousand times more efficacious to bathe in the Ganges at the confluence of the three rivers—the Ganges, the Jumna and the mythological Saraswati—than in ordinary Melas.

Thus, for many, attendance at this festival became the fulfillment of a lifelong dream and desire, and they came from all over India. Untold numbers traveled several thousand miles, as did the Chaudharis, carrying their provisions with them to camp out on the riverbank, for days or sometimes weeks. They came by boat down the Ganges and the Jumna; crammed onto trains that chugged across the landscape at a snail's pace, sitting up on third-class benches day and night. They walked—some for as long as six weeks—to reach the sacred spot.

Families brought little children. The aged, who were barely able to walk, came leaning on younger family members, or inching themselves in agony towards their goal. Some dreamed of being carried away on the bosom of Mother Ganges to eternal oblivion. It had often been said that those who died at that sacred spot attained immediate salvation.

The Indian government, however, did everything in its power to maintain safety and order. At this particular Mela they provided thousands of police, fully staffed field hospitals, and even required cholera inoculations before the pilgrims entered the area.

However, the crowds inexplicably swelled, and by the 3rd of February, the most auspicious day of the season, an estimated two to five million people crowded into an eighty acre area.

The scene resembled a refugee camp. Pilgrims lived in grass huts, tent-like structures, and tin shanties. Priests and "pandas" (Brahmins who performed various functions for the bathers, such as providing sandalwood, mantras, horoscopes, watching clothing while they bathed, etc.) had special flags mounted on poles to identify their locations.

A pall of smoke hung over the camp, redolent with the aroma of dung fires and hot spicy foods being cooked over them. Women busied themselves with "housekeeping"—washing clothes in the river and hanging their soggy saris to dry on bamboo poles stuck in the sand.

Beggars lined the road to the bathing site—the lepers, maimed, deformed, and the charlatans. Some were carried by their "owners," who fought over the best spots to catch the attention of the pilgrims, who added to their merits by giving food and rice to those who begged.

A special area was set aside for the Sadhus—groups of holy men who were both feared and revered by the pilgrims. Sadhus frequently traveled in bands, begging for their livelihood. They dressed in orange loincloths (some went naked) and carried swords and tridents, which many believed had power to destroy or place a curse on them.

It was not possible for everyone to enter the water at the most propitious moment—which was often in the middle of the night or at the break of dawn. So thousands strained forward hour after hour towards the water's edge, and out to the sandbank which formed the most sacred bathing spot in all of India.

Once immersed, the pilgrims splashed themselves with the polluted liquid, dipped water with their hands to drink, and allowed the holy river to trickle through their fingers. If they bathed at night or in the early dawn, they seemed oblivious to the bitter cold.

They offered flowers and coconut shells which they'd purchased from pandas at inflated prices. As they raised their hands to their foreheads in worship, their faces reflected peace and even ecstasy. For they believed this one act could build up merit to escape the eternal trap of "birth-death-birth-death." This perfect Kumbh Mela in 1954 was said to shorten the cycle by 1000 years.

Yet, tragedy turned this Kumbh Mela into a horrible death trap. Anand read a fuller account of the events the next day in the paper.

The story reported that 356 people were killed and 2000 injured in a stampede. A government commission was looking into the cause. Few other details were given. Anand wondered if his parents would have seen what had happened.

At first there was no premonition that they had been involved; the odds were, after all, very small. Besides, he and his father had unfinished business to settle as soon as he returned. Anand was marshalling his arguments, using the best logic he could muster, to prepare his case for the Shastri. Hadn't he said if Anand could convince him of the truth of Christianity, he too would seek the Christian God? Yet, as the days passed with no word from his parents, a gnawing concern began to surface.

And then one afternoon late in February, Anand returned home to find the house filled with relatives, wailing and crying. Crouched on the floor, his hands in his face, was one of those who had traveled to Allahabad with his parents.

For a moment, Anand stood unobserved in the doorway. But even before his aunt rushed to throw her arms around him, he knew. His parents had died in the stampede at Allahabad.

He sank to the floor as though struck. Even in that moment of horror his heart cried to God, to hold him strong, not to let him falter in his faith.

He must have sat for hours surrounded by the grieving family. He didn't hear the priests who'd been called in recite mantras monotonously over the sacred fires. He hardly noticed when they smeared sandalwood on his forehead as part of the ritual.

It was as though he were paralyzed. Later he would remember the horrible story his relative told—and every detail was a knife twisting in his heart.

No one could say exactly what happened, and there were as many versions of the tragedy as observers who told it, though certain aspects were clear.

So many people had crowded into a small space that it was difficult even to breathe. Families were separated by the pushing and shoving humanity, frantic to reach the waters in time. Children torn from their parents arms screamed in terror. Fist fights broke out as impatient pilgrims tried to push ahead.

How the stampede started is uncertain. Some say a herd of elephants bringing pilgrims to the Mela ran amok.

More commonly it is said that a procession of Sadhus caused the tragedy as they came from their special camp area, leading ornately decorated elephants. A group of naked men led the procession, carrying their swords and tridents.

The auspicious moment for bathing was almost at hand, and the Sadhus believed they should be privileged to enter the waters first. When the crowd did not break to allow them passage, they began brandishing their tridents, which people believe have power to bring down fire on them. Panic stricken, the pilgrims at the front turned back to get out of the Sadhus' way. Those behind continued to push forward. The ground was slippery from the previous night's rain. People slipped and fell, only to be trampled on by others surging forward.

Beggars who were immobile were crushed to pulp; others were pushed into the deep waters, where they drowned if they couldn't swim.

Yet the crowd was so great that those in back had no idea of what was happening. They continued to push forward, eager to reach the waters as close to the propitious moment as possible. It was only as they neared the screaming melee that they realized—too late—that they were being sucked into a human crushing machine.

Anand's relative could not explain how his life was spared and Aunt and Uncle and Pushpanjali were trampled to death. The last he'd seen them they had linked hands to keep from being separated.

Hours later, after the police had at last been able to restore order, he began searching through the bodies. A deathly hush, broken only by weeping, hung over the stunned masses. Loudspeakers broke into the silence to announce the names of missing people and how to contact their distraught relatives.

After hours of searching among the dead and dying, Anand's relative found the badly mangled bodies of the Chaudharis, and he was able to see that they received a proper cremation.

The stench of rotting corpses and the pungent smoke from cremating bodies hung over the riverbank for three days and nights. Though the official death toll remained at less than 500, those who were there believed as many as 5000 were lost. For days Anand relived the scene in his mind, until he believed he was going insane. Locking himself in his room, he could not speak to anyone. The family honored his grief.

Over and over Anand asked himself, "Why?" He couldn't understand why God allowed this terrible thing to happen. Before he'd become a Christian, Anand had everything—a good home, servants, a car, comfortable living in a wealthy area of Bombay.

Now it was all gone. Anand was beside himself. He felt as if he were going insane. Everyone he loved was gone—his parents, his sister; and his aunt and uncle had rejected him. He was totally alone.

"Yet strangely enough," Anand would write later, "even in those first days of shock, the gracious words of Christ came to give me my only real comfort: 'Let not your heart be troubled, ye believe in God, believe also in me.' These words came to me again and again, when everyone else was against me.

"Somehow I began to feel that I had been so severely separated from all that I loved in order that I might love Him more. The feeling came to me, insisting that I must leave everything, including college and my degree, and dedicate my life to serve the living and the true God."

Anand doesn't recall how many days he sat in shock in his room, but after some time his uncle knocked and called him to meet with the family.

A solemn group awaited him in the sitting room, including the priests and several members of the community judges.

Each caste community has a group of elders who make up the caste court, laying down rules for marriage, arbitrating family disputes, excommunicating erring members, etc. Anand's family had presented his case to the members of the court, or panchayat, for their arbitration.

The spokesman came directly to the point. "Your treachery in seeking the Christian God has angered the gods. We believe you are the cause of your parents' death!"

Anand sat numbly listening to their diatribe. They threatened that he would have to leave his aunt and uncle's house unless he gave up any contacts with Christianity. He would have to go through a lengthy rite of purification to be reinstated as a priest.

If he refused to leave, his foster parents would also be excommunicated.

There was no doubt in Anand's mind that he would never return to Hinduism. The more difficult question at the moment was where to go. He had only known two homes—the one in Goa at the temple, and this gracious home of his aunt and uncle for the past twelve years.

After a few days Anand told his aunt he was going back to Goa. As the only remaining son it was his duty to take care of his father's property and possessions.

Alone in his first-class compartment, Anand once again took that jarring train ride back to Goa. He was oblivious to the lush rice paddies and stately coconut palms of the verdant countryside.

Mechanically he hired a taxi. He spoke to no one as he waited for the dilapidated ferry to take him across the river less than a mile to Dhargal. His heart beat in his throat as he drove under the white cement arch which marked the entrance to his village. Nothing had changed—yet everything had.

He left the taxi outside the temple entrance and entered the familiar courtyard.

What memories poured over him as he stepped into the little tile and mud house at the back gate of the temple property. It was just as he remembered it—his mother's cooking utensils right where she'd left them; the water jug, her saris folded neatly, and the sleeping mats in the bedroom.

His parents had lived so simply compared with their rich relatives in Bombay. The only wealth was in his father's books, which were still on the shelves as he'd remembered them when he was a boy—the Upanishads, the Vedas, the Gita.

What should he do with these things? They were part of another life, gone forever—not only because his parents were dead, but because of his new life in Christ.

Anand walked into his father's coconut grove. It was like a park, with the towering palms softly waving in the afternoon breeze. It looked good—the villagers had kept it well. The trees were heavy with fruit and ready for harvest.

What should he do with this property that was now his? He had no money, and was sure his aunt and uncle would never give him any more. He would need to find a place to live and food to eat until he found a job of some kind. He'd never worked a day in his life, and India's job market was almost impossible to break into without proper connections. He could hardly imagine himself working for three or four rupees a day doing manual labor.

But even as he mulled over these problems, he remembered the words he'd read in Matthew just before he left Bombay: "Go sell what thou hast and give to the poor and thou shalt have treasure in heaven, and come, follow me." He knew God would take care of him.

The decision made, he went to the villagers who'd rented the land from his father for a share of the crop. They were still in shock from the news of the Shastri's death.

"I'm leaving here now; I won't be taking any of the things out of the house. Divide them up among the people of the village who need them."

"And you and the others who worked in the coconut grove can have it—just share it fairly among yourselves."

He didn't add that he could not take for himself anything that was gained through the temple worship—and everything his father had had come from the gifts to the gods.

And so he returned to Panjim, the capitol of Goa, penniless

(except for a few rupees cash in his pocket), homeless, friendless, and directionless.

He knew no one who could help him. He'd never met another Christian besides Joseph; he'd never been in a church. He was only in God's hands for Him to do with as He pleased.

On a Sunday night in April, he sat disconsolately in the lobby of a hotel in Panjim that had seen better days. It was hot and sticky and the ceiling fan in the lobby offered little relief from his sweltering room. Music blared from a radio. He didn't pay much attention, though radios were not common in India and only public places or very wealthy homes had them.

Into his meandering mind a name broke out of the radio that caught his attention. The voice spoke about Jesus Christ. Anand moved closer so that he could listen to this incredible coincidence. But in his heart he knew it wasn't that.

At the end of the program the announcer gave the name and address of a Bible school in Jhansi in the province of Uttar Pradesh, 1200 miles north of Bombay.

A school just to study the Bible? He'd had no idea such a place existed. He yearned to know more about the Bible. He didn't even own a complete one. But even the little he'd read convinced him it was a book worthy of his most intense study. It was the one source and direction for his new life.

At that moment he made a critical decision. He would go to the Bible school in Jhansi.

And so one more time Anand returned to the stately house on Malabar Hill in Bombay. As he pushed open the wrought iron gate, a pang of sadness overwhelmed him. For so many years this had been the place of refuge and comfort for him; a loving family had provided for his every need. He'd known respect and honor as he'd moved proudly among the family and caste community.

But he knew his decision to go to a Bible school would be the ultimate break with his past. He'd come back to pack his clothes and books and take his farewell from his aunt and uncle.

Stepping into the front hall his eyes fell on the god shelf built into a special alcove where burning incense filled the room with the familiar sweet scent. The blank stare of the family god, garlanded with flowers and surrounded by offerings, belied the power that ornately decorated image had held over him. It seemed a lifetime since he'd last bowed before that painted deity and chanted ritual mantras. If only he could free those he loved from its power.

Once more he returned to his room overlooking the sea. He wanted to wash after the dust and grime of the train, and put on clean clothes before looking for his aunt.

As he came back into the front hall, his aunt appeared in the doorway, her usually gentle, smiling face, drawn and tense. She would have passed him by, but Anand stopped her.

"Auntie, I'm going to be leaving soon—I just came back to get my things."

For a moment her face softened. "Where are you going Anand?" The pain and love in her voice tore at him; he knew his aunt really loved and cared for him. He had taken the place in her heart of the son she'd never had.

"Are you still determined to carry on with this foolishness? Can't you see you're throwing your life away, as well as hurting the whole family? Here you have everything your uncle and I can give you. You've a successful future ahead of you. Give up the idea of being a Christian," she pled. "The members of the panchayat have already said they would reinstate you."

Anand just shook his head. "I can't go back, Auntie. I know now that Jesus Christ is the only true God. I can't go back to worshiping idols."

"Then what do you intend doing?"

"I'm not sure, Auntie. I've heard about a school that teaches the Bible up in Jhansi. If I'm going to serve God, I must know more about the Christian scriptures, so I'm going to try to find this school."

His aunt drew herself up to her full height, anger pouring over her face. "If that's your final decision, you can just turn around and leave right now. You'll not take one thing from this house. You'll go just as you're standing here. Go—go as you are. But one day you'll come back, because you can't survive alone after living the kind of life we've given you here."

For a moment Anand stared at her, trying to think of something to say that would change her mind. He hadn't expected her to sympathize with his plans, nor help him financially. He had a few personal possessions in his room that he could have sold. But he hadn't expected that she'd turn him out of the house like this!

However, Anand saw that his aunt meant exactly what she'd said.

He was to leave just as he was. He had put on a pair of casual slacks and slipped his bare feet into thongs after his bath—hardly suitable for a long journey.

In his pocket was a copy of the Gospels and a few rupees; he had no idea how far they would get him towards his destination.

Painfully he recalled his mother's parting words, "If this vision is real, then you must live by faith, and your God will provide whatever you need."

Without another word he turned and left the house to begin his journey of faith.

Part II

Servant of the King
1954-1985

9

"Just Another Floater"

Back at Victoria Station, Anand waited in the queue at the ticket window to get information about the next train to Jhansi. He discovered that he barely had enough money in his pocket to purchase a third-class ticket, with a few rupees to spare. Anand had never traveled anything but first class since he'd lived with his aunt and uncle. They usually had a compartment to themselves, and if they traveled overnight, would pull berths down so that each person had his/her own bed.

Anand had often been irritated at the masses of people that crowded into the carriages behind first class, so that they hung out the windows, and sometimes even clambered up on the roof. He wondered how people could stand to travel in such crowded conditions, without water or space to move around, especially in the heat of the day. He was going to find out.

Before boarding the train, he looked for a newspaper. The thought of traveling 24 hours without having anything to read was worse than being without food. In the bookstand his eyes fell on a small book entitled *Everyman's Bible,* which contained short readings from the whole Bible. He couldn't resist buying it, even though it left him almost penniless.

He'd never had to practice the aggressive pushing and shoving that was a way of life in over-populated India. With his natural reserve and genteel nature, he almost missed the train to Jhansi, as others pushed ahead of him into the already crowded coach.

But somehow he managed to jump on the train before it began to pull out of the station. The only place left to sit was to crawl up on the wooden ledge which was meant to serve as a top bunk. Four other men were already crouching cross-legged on the ledge, so they didn't dangle their legs over the edge into the faces of the passengers below. But they were most comfortable sitting in that customary manner and good-naturedly moved over to make room for him.

As the hours passed the heat became more oppressive. Mercifully, Anand hardly noticed the strong aroma of unwashed sweaty bodies and untrained babies.

Mothers brought out little metal containers with cold curries and dal, thrusting morsels into the mouths of their children with almost dainty precision, or modestly nursed their screaming infants by drawing their colorful saris over their breasts.

Vendors moved up and down along the open windows at the train's frequent stops from one tiny village to the next. Some boarded the train, loudly hawking their wares—peanuts, fruit, tea, sweetmeats, bread, and cakes. Anand spent his last rupee to buy a cup of tea and a few biscuits for his supper.

In the darkness bodies swayed against each other. Some seemed to sleep soundly, oblivious of their discomfort, but for Anand there was no sleep.

About one a.m. on Friday, the 15th of April, the train pulled into Jhansi, and Anand wearily began walking along the platform—the longest in India, he was to learn later—towards the station.

But the lack of food and sleep had taken its toll, and he realized that he could go no farther without rest.

Today as he looks back at that morning, he still can't believe how he could have brought himself to spread his newspaper out on the cement platform and stretch out to sleep in the midst of the moving mass of people in the station.

He awoke some time later, embarrassed to find himself lying in a public place like an outcaste. But no one paid a bit of attention to him as he picked up his newspaper and brushed off his grubby clothes. Chagrined, he felt the two day stubble on his chin.

For several hours Anand wandered around the town of Jhansi, asking in his rusty Hindi for directions to the Bible school. Most people had never heard of it, and looked rather suspiciously at this stranger whose accent betrayed him as a south Indian.

Though Anand was fluent in several languages, he was probably the least comfortable in Hindi. His father had taught him Hindi and Sanskrit, and his mother tongue, Bengali. Since the language of the area where he grew up was Konkani, that had become the common language spoken in the home. In Bombay his relatives spoke Marathi, and he had become very fluent in that as well.

But the language of educated Indians was English, and in recent years he had spoken it almost exclusively. So Anand could speak at least five of the fourteen official languages of India, but his Hindi was heavy with a southern accent.

He finally found someone who knew the location of the Bible school. It was just two miles from the railway station, but Anand had wandered around for hours trying to find it.

"Just take a turn on Gwalior Road and you'll come to a stone wall," his informant told him. "The entrance has a sign that says C.P. Mission Compound."

Anand found a gatekeeper sitting in the shade of a tree and asked where the Bible school was.

"Just go up to the road to the church and turn left. You'll see the school straight ahead."

Anand's heart was in turmoil as he trudged up the dusty road towards the school. By now he was beginning to feel weak from lack of food and water, though the thought of begging for these did not even enter his mind. His mother need not have reminded him that a Brahmin does not stretch his hand out to beg from strangers—it was ingrained in his very makeup.

But, what was he doing here at this Christian school—a foreign mission? How could he study here without any money for fees or books? Was he going to beg for his keep from foreigners?

But he reminded himself, these were followers of Jesus. They must know something of His compassion and concern for the poor and suffering. In his reading of the Gospels this had been the compelling characteristic which had set the Lord Christ apart from the Hindu deities; His unselfish love demonstrated a moral perfection Anand had never seen in all his studies of Hindu scriptures.

Even in those rudimentary stages of his Christian experience, however, Anand's expectation was not to find moral perfection in Christians—but to study the perfect God in the Christian Scriptures.

There was an unusual quiet on the compound that puzzled Anand. The only sound in the hot afternoon stillness was the buzzing of the flies, and the occasional call of birds as they winged across the trees. There was no one in sight.

Anand stepped onto the broad veranda running the length of the school building. Strange. He knocked on the screen door, but there was no reply. He crouched down in the shade of the veranda, determined to wait until somebody appeared.

After just a few minutes, a young man came around the corner. When he saw Anand he asked, "Where have you come from?" Anand explained that he'd come from Bombay and was looking for the principal of the Bible school.

The boy explained that everyone was at the church. "Why don't you come along—you can see Rev. McKay after the service."

It was only later that Anand learned that he had arrived at the Canadian Presbyterian Mission on Good Friday, when services were held from nine to three to remember the death of Jesus.

His first church service was a bewildering experience. The inside of the church was very plain. It didn't look anything like a temple. The walls were whitewashed, without ornament or pictures. Instead of an altar up in front, there was a simple wooden cross. Of course, Anand thought, that's to remind them of how Jesus was killed. There was one familiar sight—the pile of shoes outside the door. He kicked his thongs off before entering this holy place.

As he walked in, everyone was standing and singing. At first he couldn't pick out the Hindi words, but gradually he realized they were singing about Jesus' love in dying on the cross.

He stood awkwardly at the back, wondering if there was some gesture or ritual he should be following? Should he have brought an offering? He saw no evidence of gifts; there was no incense or fire. Just one vase of flowers decorated the table at the front.

Then he noticed a man standing behind a box who motioned everyone to sit down. Quickly Anand sank to the floor at the back of the benches. Fortunately he'd noticed that men and women were sitting on separate sides of the church.

"I couldn't understand what they were doing," Anand recalls. "I had never seen people sitting together like that, singing, listening to messages, one after another."

The Indian students and children sat cross-legged on the floor, while adults sat on benches at the back. There were ten or twelve Europeans in the church as well. Anand assumed they were missionaries. He had heard about their work in India, mainly in a derogatory way in the Communist books he'd read. The men took turns reading from the Bible—Anand recognized the stories they were reading of the suffering and death of Jesus. They were like music to his ears. For the first time since Joseph's death he heard another human being share the beautiful story of Jesus. His heart almost burst with joy and healing after the lonely months of suffering he'd come through.

The spell was somewhat broken when the service closed. "I was just standing in the corner there; I didn't know whom to speak to because they were all speaking among themselves, and nobody cared about me, or even looked at me," Anand recalls.

"But then one of the missionaries came up to me—I learned it was the principal, Angus McKay—and he asked, 'Where have you come from? You aren't from this area."

When Angus MacKay learned that Anand had come all the way from Bombay, he took him along to his bungalow where they could talk further.

While Rev. McKay listened with interest to Anand's story, the other missionaries were skeptical when they heard it.

Mr. Russell Self, one of the missionaries on the station, admits, "Most of us didn't give any credence to his story, that his folks were wiped out in the Mela and that he'd come to study the Bible. We had so many loafers passing through since we were near the railway. Some had some very well constructed stories."

Mrs. McKay was even more forthright. "We rejected him. His story was, oh, so familiar; we'd heard them all. And from what we could gather, he was a Brahmin and we didn't take non-Christians in our Bible school."

But while other missionaries found Anand's story "too much to believe," Angus McKay had seen beyond the self-controlled dispassionate exterior into the heart of a young man seeking truth.

Inviting him into the bungalow for a cup of tea and the usual cakes and sandwiches that were served in mid-afternoon at the mission, Rev. McKay urged Anand to tell his story.

He and his wife had been at Allahabad at the time of the Mela to distribute literature and do personal evangelism among the crowd. They had seen the bodies brought up from the river bank to be laid out for identification. This experience enabled him to identify more personally with Anand's grief.

For several hours the two men talked, and McKay was impressed with Anand's openness to Christ, even though he knew so little of the teachings of Christianity.

When Mr. McKay found that Anand owned only the Gospels, he went to his study and returned with a black hardcover book.

"Here, take this Hindi Bible. This is the complete Scriptures of Christianity. The Old Testament is the history of God's people as He prepares the way for Jesus the Messiah. And the rest of the New Testament more fully explains the teachings of Christ and what the church is."

Anand took the book with both his hands, then raised them to his forehead in a gesture of gratitude. This is what he'd come for. Now he could study the truth to his heart's content.

To McKay and others at the mission who came to know Anand well in the months ahead, Anand was a seeker, and they believe he was converted at the school. Later McKay would write, "I was profoundly impressed by Anand's intense seriousness and genuine sincerity, and his readiness to accept Jesus Christ as Saviour and Lord, and dedicate his life wholeheartedly to Christ and His service."

But Anand says he had truly accepted Jesus as his Lord that evening at the seashore in Bombay. He just didn't know the terminology or the doctrine.

Rev. McKay arranged for Anand to stay in the boys hostel. This was the beginning of the spring holidays and most of the students and staff would be gone for the month. However, two orphans who had no home to go to stayed behind with Anand. It seemed quite natural to him that they should cook for him, while he spent hours in reading the Bible and meditation.

When the school reopened, Anand began attending classes. But the next few months were a painful time in his life. His heart was still raw from his terrible loss, and he found it difficult to enter into the give and take of student life on the compound.

The students looked at Anand with suspicion and awe. Most of them had come from low-caste backgrounds; many were second generation Christians who had never met or interacted with a Brahmin before. He was obviously well educated, versed in philosophy, languages, history—while most of them had completed only a few years of primary education and knew little or no English. He was a light-skinned Aryan; most of them were from the darker Dravidian strains, looked down upon for their color.

Unfortunately, many second and third generation Christians even today find it difficult to accept recent converts from Hinduism and Islam. The students were simply reflecting the ethos of the Christian community in general.

Though Anand had only one set of clothes, which he washed at night and put back on again in the morning, he carried himself with an air of dignity and self-confidence that bespoke of wealth and position. They considered him arrogant.

But for Anand, this was one of the loneliest periods of his life. "Nobody in Jhansi would talk to me," he recalls. "The students wouldn't come near me. They couldn't believe I was sincere. I guess they thought I was some sort of spy."

Yet, in his ardent daily Bible study, he found new promises to cling to that soothed his lonely heart. Over and over the Holy Spirit whispered, "I will never leave you nor forsake you."

Anand found it difficult to perform the menial tasks assigned to him such as cleaning and carrying water from the well. After all, these were suitable for peasants, not students, he reasoned. He was here to study and prepare himself for serving God. But students and faculty alike misunderstood his attitude and thought him lazy.

Mr. McKay, however, continued to take time for this intriguing young man and frequently called him up to the bungalow for a visit. He was impressed with his grasp of languages and his perception of spiritual truth.

Several months after Anand's arrival at Jhansi, McKay revealed to him why he had accepted him when others questioned his sincerity.

"When I was praying that morning before you came, the Lord definitely told me that a young man would come, and that I should accept him," McKay confessed. "The Lord prepared my heart, so that when I saw you in the service I came up to you immediately. And now it's confirmed that you are the person about whom the Lord was speaking."

Anand was finally accepted as a student in the Bible school and he applied himself with diligence to the study of the Bible. But he was still lonely. His years of study and meditation had inured him to solitude and reinforced his independence. But the sudden wrenching of all that he held dear, and his new relationship with his compassionate Lord, made him long for fellowship. His talks with Mr. McKay and others on the staff, who were by now accepting him as a sincere and gifted student, were a help. But he needed to begin to relate to other Indian Christians; he needed friends and someone to talk to.

By the end of the year a few of the students had broken down their reserve to include him in their activities. One afternoon Nelson Nathanael suggested that Anand join him as he visited his aunt and uncle, the Jacobs, who worked for one of the missionary families on the compound.

As they approached the caretakers flat in the school hostel, a small gentle-looking woman appeared in the doorway. Her round dark face lit up in a brilliant smile of welcome, which included the young stranger.

10

The First Steps of Service

Anand frequently found himself drawn to the Jacobs' home. At first he came only when Nathanael invited him. But when the Jacobs moved from the hostel to a tiny two-room cottage just outside the gate of the compound, it was easy for Anand to drop in on his way to or from town.

While at the Jacobs' home, Anand would watch and listen in amazement. The family, sitting comfortably on the mats on the dirt floor, filled the small front room of the cottage with laughter and happy chatter. The girls would serve tea. Mrs. Jacob would try to include him in the lively conversation, but he found it difficult to join in the happy banter.

The Jacob family was originally from south India, and were darker skinned than most north Indians. Their Hindu ancestors had been outcastes.

Anand learned that Mr. Jacob had worked as a housekeeper for one of the missionary families on the compound. But his love for the Lord and self-taught knowledge of the Word soon became evident, and he frequently traveled as an evangelist with the Muchans, a Canadian missionary family. Sometimes his whole family would go with him; they would sing and play their tambourines in the services.

The eight children had all been brought up here on the Canadian Presbyterian Mission compound in Jhansi and were able to attend the mission schools.

One of the older daughters had married, and the other was a Bible woman in the mission hospital. The two younger girls, Sarla and Kusum, were still in school, as were the two young boys.

It was not the size of the family that amazed Anand—Indian families often have eight children or more—but the close-knit relationships astonished him.

There was laughter and singing. Sometimes Sarla and Kusum

would sing a duet—"a song composed by Mummy," he was told. Subadra Jacob had made inquiries about the reserved young man who sat so quietly in the corner of her home, saying little, just sitting and listening. When she learned of the tragedy that had precipitated his coming to Jhansi, she began praying for him every day. She learned from her missionary friends that he was not included in the general life of the school and that the students found it hard to get close to him.

Anand could not explain the feelings of comfort and acceptance that came over him as he sat in the adobe hut on the mud floor of these simple outcaste people. Sometimes he spent an evening when the whole family was together. Sometimes he came just to sit and chat with Mrs. Jacob. He found her easy to talk with, a ready and compassionate listener.

In later years he would describe her as "sweet-hearted and helpful, someone whom everybody loved." She often traveled with her husband to the military camps where he preached, or visited local areas with one of the missionaries to tell Bible stories or teach the children songs. But primarily she invested love, prayer, and time in her eight children, all of whom continued as strong and faithful Christians after they left home.

Subadra listened and asked questions as Anand began peeling off the layers of independence that he had built up over many years. Over and over he recounted the story of his parents, describing their dreams and ambitions for him, their blind commitment to Hinduism, and their fatal trip to Allahabad.

It was as if he wanted to pull the subject out of his heart and examine it from every angle; to assure himself once again that there was nothing he could have done to prevent their deaths.

And Subadra listened and comforted—and prayed. Anand found in that simple little home a family that accepted and loved him, and a faith that matched what he'd been reading about in Scripture. In a sense, God had given him another foster mother to replace the two mothers he'd lost, and the love and respect of younger brothers to take the place of his own.

By this time the missionary staff had recognized Anand's unusual gifts and abilities. And when in the fall of 1955 a Brethren missionary, Dennis Clark of the Christian Literature Institute, came to Jhansi for a convention, Anand was asked to help with the literature table.

Through this Anand came to Mr. Clark's attention.

As a result, Mr. Clark gave Anand some translation work to do, and was so impressed with his linguistic ability that he asked him to consider working for him after he completed Bible school.

Angus McKay, on the other hand, believed that Anand should go on to further his Bible training. The course at Jhansi covered only two years' study, and was at a rather low level. McKay felt that abilities should be more finely tuned.

Though he still had a year before he completed his studies at Jhansi, Anand now began thinking of future plans, and how he could best serve the eternal God who had so obviously chosen him.

Anand and Mrs. Jacob discussed his future often, and it became clear that one issue that should be settled soon was to find a suitable wife. Mrs. Jacob recognized what Anand would not admit to himself. He was lonely and needed a family of his own.

If his parents had lived, they would have arranged a suitable match once his education was completed. They would have carefully evaluated the girl's family status, her color, character, and the ability to pay dowry. His father would have sought auspicious signs in astrology. Both families would have met to discuss arrangements and agree on financial provisions. Anand would probably not have met his future wife until the day of the formal engagement ceremony.

Most Hindu parents still arrange marriages for their children in this way. The Sunday papers in large cities have several pages of matrimonial ads for brides and grooms.

Parents feel obligated to find a mate for their sons because in India a man without a wife is considered an incomplete being. Also, a son is needed to perform the last duties in connection with the parents' funeral and insure their access to the Abode of Bliss after death.

It was for this reason Anand's aunt and uncle had adopted him, and if he had stayed with them, he would have been the heir to his uncle's estate upon his uncle's death.

The Hindu scriptures also explain the urgency of marriage for a woman. The Padmapurana states, "There is no other god on earth for a woman than her husband. The most excellent of all good works that she can do is to seek to please him by manifesting perfect obedience to him." Many orthodox Hindu wives live their lives in total servitude towards their husbands.

But Anand had seen the difference in Christian marriages, and he realized the importance of finding a Christian partner to serve God with him. Yet he had no preparation or background to find a wife himself; and the Jacobs were now his surrogate parents, so he turned to them.

It came as no surprise to him when Mrs. Jacob suggested that Anand marry Sarla, even though she was eight years his junior and had not yet completed high school.

Her soft, gentle nature appealed to Anand, and he believed she demonstrated potential for becoming a faithful, godly wife. Above all, he respected Mrs. Jacob's opinion, and knew she wanted the best for him. He agreed to marry Sarla when she completed school.

In June 1956, Anand finished his course at Jhansi. He was anxious to become involved in ministry right away, and moved to Delhi to work with Dennis Clark in the Christian Literature Institute. He was put in charge of translation and editing for the publishing house. At one point he was involved in a newspaper evangelism project for the Bible Society, in which a new translation of the Hindi Gospel of Mark was printed in a Delhi paper over a period of four months.

Anand began teaching a Bible class to a group of people who responded to the newspaper project. A number of people came to Christ, including Dr. Goel, who is today coordinator of evangelists and manager of a Christian school in Bharatapur, as part of Anand's ministry.

It was in this Bible class that Anand recognized his gift for teaching and discipling, and God began to stir his heart for a wider ministry beyond editing and translation.

Sarla was now in Bible school, so she and Anand only saw each other at school holidays when Anand would return to his "home" in Jhansi. But very soon after Sarla left for school she began suffering poor health. She tried to ignore the pain and weakness for months. But finally, early in 1957 she was sent home and was taken to the mission hospital for treatment.

After months of testing the doctors found inexplicable abdominal cysts that had to be removed surgically. Sarla seemed to come through the operation well. But when Anand was finally able to visit Jhansi, Mrs. Jacob took him aside to speak to him before he visited Sarla in the hospital. He could tell from her face that something was wrong.

"Son, the doctor has given us a report on Sarla that I must tell you.

The cysts caused a lot of internal damage, and though they have corrected the problem so that she should be perfectly healthy, it looks as though she will never be able to bear children."

"I know what this must mean to you," she paused. "If you want to cancel the marriage, we'll understand."

But even though the news came as a shock to Anand, his answer was unequivocal, "If we'd been married when this surgery took place, I wouldn't have left her. So since I've promised before the Lord to marry her, I will keep my promise."

Even in that moment he recalled his own mother urging him to choose one woman, marry her, and not go after other girls.

Later Anand spoke to the doctor himself, who verified what Mrs. Jacob had said, though she admitted to Anand that the Lord could still do a miracle.

Sarla herself never lost hope that after their marriage the Lord would hear their prayers and give them a child. But there was always a sense of willingness on both their parts for God's will, whatever He granted.

And so in 1958, Angus McKay served as intermediary for Anand and the official engagement was arranged with her parents.

Now Mrs. Jacob allowed the young couple time to sit together and talk and plan, something generally unheard of in traditional Indian families. But Anand and Sarla were given more freedom, no doubt through the influence of Western missionaries with whom her parents had worked for many years.

Though they were learning to appreciate each other, the road to love was not smooth.

Anand's expectations, naturally, came from his Brahmin background. A decent Indian woman didn't laugh and talk with men. Though he had enjoyed the warmth and laughter of the Jacob home as a visitor, now he wasn't sure he wanted his wife to take part in such free social interaction.

"I had not moved in the Christian community, and the intimacy and mixing up really bothered me," he admits now. "That was not my background."

He disapproved when Sarla demonstrated affection for her brothers. In his childhood he recalled that Pushbanjali was allowed to touch him only once a year, on a special day set aside for brothers, when she placed a garland around his neck. Yet Sarla would laugh and pat her brother on the back, or lean against him when talking to him.

When he mentioned these things to Sarla, she was heartbroken, sure that Anand could not love her if she displeased him so.

Her mother wisely counseled her, "Listen to Anand and try to please him. As you get to know him better, you'll understand why he expects you to behave as he does."

And indeed, Sarla did learn that when Anand criticized her for not covering her face with her sari, or for sitting near him in public, it had nothing to do with his love for her. And he in turn learned to relax and enjoy the freedom of relationships that the Jacob family had developed.

But it didn't happen overnight.

The year 1959 brought two major changes into Anand's life. He left the literature work to begin teaching in a new Bible school, the Delhi Bible Institute started by Robert Duff, a Brethren missionary. And he and Sarla were married on the mission compound in Jhansi on the 30th of December, 1959, and moved to Delhi.

Sarla remembers the excitement of having their own room above a garage, and the first testings of their faith. There was no regular salary promised, so they received funds only as gifts came in.

"One day we had used up everything that had come in," she recalls. "The rent was due, and we didn't have a rupee left. We didn't even have food in the house. We prayed together that night for God to provide for our needs.

"The next morning Anand took the shopping basket when he left for work. I asked him, 'Where are you going to get food?'

"He told me he was going to Mr. Duff and that he believed the Lord would provide the money that day. When Anand arrived at the house, Mr. Duff had an envelope with 300 rupees that he had received for us."

So God began teaching in these simple ways that Sarla and Anand could trust Him for their day-to-day needs; for He would soon be asking them to trust Him for their dreams.

11
Miracles in Toronto

"But I have to have the passport and sanction form right away. I just found out that my plane leaves at two this afternoon," insisted Anand.

Rarely was Anand as close to anger as he was facing the indifferent official at the Reserve Bank of India. He had been given to believe that everything was in order with his ticket to Toronto, Canada. But when he'd arrived at the Indian Airlines office that morning he'd been told that the ticket could not be written until he was given a bank clearance stamped in his passport. And more seriously, the night flight to Bombay had been cancelled, and he would have to take the afternoon flight if he were to make his connection in Bombay for the plane to London.

Now Anand had run into the usual civil servants' indifference; his personal pleas and desperate circumstances made no difference. Perhaps a few rupees under the counter might have given the official some inspiration to act, but Anand had never used bribery to achieve his ends.

"I'm afraid it will take some time, Mr. Chaudhari. The officer has many others ahead of you," the clerk reiterated.

"I'll just wait here until he signs it," Anand responded stubbornly.

Anand watched the clerk disappear into an inner office, bearing his brand new passport and a sheaf of documents Anand had filled out. Anand turned and forced his way out of the crowd of pushing bodies around him, who were also holding documents in their hands for the harried clerk's attention.

"If everyone of the people waiting outside the manager's door had deposited a paper on his desk for his attention, I could be here for the rest of the day," thought Anand. He glanced at his watch; it was almost 11 a.m.

Anand noticed a bench against the wall that had been vacated, and he dropped wearily into it, immediately withdrawing into that precious place of prayer he had learned to depend on. It was still a special delight to realize that he could converse with his God in any place, without temple, idol or ritual.

"Lord, I don't know why this hurdle has come when you've opened all the doors so far . . . ."

And almost instantaneously the Holy Spirit lifted a verse from his memory, "I have set an open door before you, and no one can shut it."

In that moment Anand relaxed, confident that his dreams would become a reality.

The dream had begun more than a year ago. Anand had become more and more frustrated with his ministry at the Delhi Bible Institute. Ever since he had come to north India he had been overwhelmed with the masses of Hindi-speaking people who were living in the same spiritual ignorance and blindness he had been. He was convinced that evangelists and pastors had to be trained in their mother tongue in order to share the teachings of Scripture effectively.

But most classes at Delhi Bible Institute were taught in English, which effectively eliminated the majority of those who Anand felt needed the training. And as more English-speaking Indians attended the institute, more and more emphasis was placed on using the English language.

During this period Anand also began broadcasting a weekly program over Far East Broadcasting Corporation, "The Immortal Voice of the Bible." There was an effort to follow up those who wrote in for correspondence courses, but he felt restricted by the goals of the missionaries who supervised him. Although there was a good working relationship, Anand was concerned that the Bible Institute was not making a greater impact on the millions of Hindi-speaking people around him. More and more his vision for how this could be done conflicted with those in charge.

Just about this time the Bible Society approached Anand to ask him to serve on the Old Testament translation committee for the new Hindi Bible.

That new opportunity added to his frustrations since he'd never been able to study Greek or Hebrew; in fact, his formal Bible training had been on a very basic level, and he felt wholly inadequate to tackle such an important task.

Thus, the idea of going overseas to study had been simmering in his heart for a number of years. Many times he and Sarla had discussed his need for more training—but they had always come to the same conclusion that it was humanly impossible.

Sarla had encouraged him to go, in spite of the fact that it would most likely mean years of separation. That thought chilled his own heart, for a deep love had developed between them, and they were truly one in their purposes and dreams.

Then one day late in 1964, Anand received a parcel of magazines from Canada. Mrs. Russell Self, one of the missionaries from Jhansi, knew Anand's insatiable love for books and reading, and had asked her friends to send him magazines.

In this bundle he found the 70th anniversary issue of the Toronto Bible College publication.

"They were giving testimonies of different people who had graduated from the Bible school and gone on to become Christian leaders," Anand recalls.

"One testimony was by Oswald J. Smith. I had read some of his books, and had, in fact, translated one, *The Man God Uses,* into Hindi. I felt if this man had been a graduate of this school, I ought to consider it."

Anand had written to Toronto Bible College (now renamed Ontario Bible College) and Columbia Bible College in South Carolina.

The reply from Columbia Bible College was discouraging; it seemed people "of color" would have a very difficult time finding a job to support themselves in the area.

But Dr. Boehmer responded positively from Toronto: "We don't have any scholarship program at our college, but we definitely feel that the Lord wants you to come. So if you are willing to come just on faith, come, and see what God will do."

It still warms Anand's heart to remember the response of his two dear missionary friends, Angus McKay and Russell Self. Not only did they encourage him, they personally offered to provide the money for the ticket.

But Sarla would have to stay behind. She bravely held back the tears as they made plans for her to return to Jhansi to stay with her parents for the next four years. What seems incomprehensible to a Western mind must be put in the perspective of Christian duty and obedience to God's call. Anand did not want to leave Sarla in India, but he realized his gifts were untrained and hence, underemployed. There was no possibility, humanly speaking, to take Sarla along. He had to go alone.

He probably could not realize the pain with which she packed up their belongings and watched him sell the few pieces of furniture they owned. The past six years in Delhi had not always been easy—she'd sensed Anand's growing restlessness and need to find his place in God's plan. And the fact that she could not give Anand the child they both so desperately wanted was a greater pain than she allowed herself to admit.

But in spite of financial struggles—and Anand's frustrations— these had been happy years in their little Delhi flat, and it wasn't easy to see it closed up.

They had gone to Jhansi to say their farewells and make arrangements for Sarla's stay with the family. As usual, Anand found the Jacobs affirming and encouraging, and he would never forget Father Jacob's prayer of blessing before they left.

Now Sarla and her brother were waiting for him back at a friend's house here in Delhi. He'd left early that morning to take care of passport and ticket, and they had planned to spend one last day together before his flight that evening.

Then the hurdles began—the change in flight to two in the afternoon; the requirement for a bank letter before the ticket could be issued; the usual red tape which threatened to hold everything up so he would miss his flight.

Yet, when Anand heard his name called by the clerk, he had utmost assurance that his documents had been taken care of.

At the counter a dumbfounded clerk stood holding his passport. "Here you are; I don't know what happened but the officer just picked up your passport and signed it."

The change in flight plans had hidden blessings. Anand barely had time to catch a taxi back to the house to pick up his things and Sarla and her brother. The prolonged agony of a day of imminent parting was mercifully cut short.

Sarla could not hold back the tears as they called Anand's flight; nor could Anand. Four years stretched out as an eternity before them, but they were both convinced this was the Lord's will and they were willing to obey.

In the months ahead Sarla wept often. It didn't help to have some "friends" tell her that Anand would forget her and marry a Canadian woman while he was overseas. But she knew his love and faithfulness could stand the test of time, and she kept herself busy teaching at the mission school in Jhansi, and waiting for his letters.

Anand was to learn how clearly God had intervened at the bank that morning when he read the papers the next day to find that Pakistan had declared war on India over the Kashmir, and all later flights to and from India had been cancelled.

The miracles continued in Toronto. Due to currency regulations, Anand arrived with $8 in his pocket—not even enough to get him to the campus.

A kindly airport official directed him to a bus which could take him to a downtown terminal in Toronto. Seeing his bewilderment, she saw to it that he got on the right bus and promised to call ahead to the terminal so they would see that he got the right transfer to the Bible school.

When Anand got off the bus in downtown Toronto a young man came towards him asking, "Are you Mr. Chow-dar-ee?" (Canadians always would have trouble pronouncing his name.)

Anand said, "Yes, I am."

"Come along with me," the young man replied, taking his suitcase. "I'll take you to the Bible college."

On the way in the car he explained, "I don't know why I stayed on because my duty here is over at six o'clock and it's almost seven now. But just as I was leaving I got this phone call to say that you were coming and that you needed to be directed to the Toronto Bible College."

He gave Anand a big understanding grin, "I'm a student at the Bible college. I take evening courses there."

In the days ahead Anand would almost take God's "special handling" for granted. Though there was no scholarship program available, Dr. Boehmer arranged for him to stay in a rented apartment across the road from the school for $8 a week until other accommodations could be found. "We're so glad you've come, Anand; we'll just look to the Lord."

Just about two weeks later, Dr. Boehmer called Anand into his office with the exciting news. "Anand, it's happened—a miracle has happened. All the money we needed for you this year—for your tuition, your lodging, your expenses—has been met. Now, you go to

Mr. Flanagan, and he'll tell you about it."

Mr. Wilson Flanagan had just recently begun working as a representative for the college. In the course of his calling upon college donors, he visited Miss Ruth Andrews. She invited him in to meet her sister and brother-in-law, the Bingleys.

During his visit, Mr. Flanagan told Miss Andrews and the Bingleys about the students who had come to the college for the new fall semester, and about the international students from Hong Kong, Singapore, and other places. He also told them about Anand's conversion and desire to serve the Lord.

Many months later the Bingleys told Anand what had happened after Mr. Flanagan left. Mr. Bingley turned to his wife and said that the Lord was speaking to him about the Indian boy who had come. And his wife said that the same thought had come to her mind.

The next morning Mr. Bingley called the school to ask how much it would cost for Anand's expenses for the year, and in a few days Mr. Flanagan went over to pick up a check from the Bingleys for the whole amount. There was even something extra "for a pair of shoes."

So began a relationship with Anand's fourth set of parents. The Bingleys were not wealthy people, but they had been wise stewards of their money. They'd recently sold a summer cottage on seven acres of land ten miles outside of Toronto, and this became their nest egg for Anand's education.

Never having had children of their own, they soon looked upon him as a son. Every Friday Anand would have supper with them, and leave with a basket of groceries to tide him over the week. Later he was given a key to the house, and freedom to come and go as he chose.

Fellow students say that Anand spoke little of his background. When he was asked to give his testimony in chapel, his voice was soft and he was painfully restrained.

Yet the depth of his experience with Christ and the unique work of God in his life was evident. Local churches began inviting this Indian student to serve their morning pulpits.

Occasionally Wilson Flanagan would travel with him to churches outside of Toronto. They often shared a motel room. One morning Wilson woke startled to see Anand sitting cross-legged on the end of the bed, staring motionless at the wall. Wilson didn't want to interrupt him, for he could see Anand was oblivious to his surroundings.

Anand's habit of meditation goes back to his early training for the priesthood. His ability to concentrate, so powerfully shaped under his father's training, was now useful in developing a strong prayer life and effective personal worship.

"I feel lifted up. It happens frequently, even today, when I'm thinking about the Lord. I go from Scripture to Scripture. I forget about my surroundings—I don't hear distracting noises. I just concentrate on the Lord."

He doesn't like to discuss his meditation habits publicly for fear they'll be misunderstood. But whenever he feels spiritually dry, with no power inside, he finds that intense meditation on the Lord and His Word recharges him.

More and more Anand found himself sharing his testimony in the churches of Ontario.

"Almost every Sunday I was out somewhere for preaching engagements in different churches. In that way the Lord helped me to look after my own personal needs, and also to have money to send to Sarla for her support," he explains.

Anand recalls one instance when he was literally down to a few dollars in his pocket. He hadn't been able to send anything to Sarla for some time, and he was concerned that she was running out of funds.

He was asked to speak at the Bethel Bible Church in Kingston, Ontario, about eighty miles from Toronto. He had just enough money to pay the one-way bus fare to the town. Sometimes churches gave him a cash gift, but more frequently they sent a check after he'd returned to school.

Yet, he set off on the Saturday afternoon with his one-way ticket, confident the Lord would supply his return fare. He was determined, however, to keep to his resolution never to ask for money for himself. This would indeed be a test of faith.

Anand spoke in both the morning and evening services. After the last service, the pastor came up to Anand and asked, "Could you come to a meeting with international students at the home of one of the members who used to be a missionary in India?"

Anand looked at his watch. "It's all right as long as I can catch the last bus back to Toronto. I have classes in the morning."

"Oh, there'll be no problem; there's a bus just before midnight. We'll see that you get on it."

But there was no mention of a gift, and as Anand spoke at the home meeting, he suppressed his uneasiness. Surely God would provide his way home. It would be a long treacherous walk on this bitterly cold and snowy night.

As he and the pastor left the house together, the pastor suddenly stopped and put his hand on Anand's shoulder. "You know Anand, I just have the feeling I should drive you back to Toronto tonight. I have a meeting there in the morning anyway."

Anand gave no indication of the relief and wonder that he felt as they started out in the driving snow. Along the way they stopped for coffee. While sitting at the table in the comforting warmth of the truck stop, the pastor reached into his pocket. "I almost forgot, I have something for you."

He handed Anand an envelope. "Our people don't usually do things like this, but one after another pressed some money into my hand for you as they left the services today."

When Anand counted the thick bundle of bills, he found $250—enough to care for him for weeks, and to send some to Sarla, too. And he didn't even have to pay for his bus ticket home.

But the money he was able to send to Sarla was never enough to fulfill her dream of going to Canada to join him. The weeks and months dragged by slowly for her, as she lived from letter to letter, trying to visualize his surroundings, wishing she could meet the Bingleys and others he talked about. She prayed for him constantly, adding the little personal "P.S." prayers about her own dream of going to Canada.

And then one day in 1968, almost three years after Anand had left, he wrote to tell her that Bingleys had offered to pay her fare to Canada: "They want to meet you." Typical of his methodical personality, all arrangements were made. The Calvary Church where Anand had been helping occasionally had a mission flat available completely furnished.

The fact that Sarla could speak very little English didn't seem to trouble her. Naturally shy and retiring, she enjoyed staying quietly in the background, as a good Indian wife should. She would cook his favorite foods (if she could find the curry and spices in Canada), care for his needs, and listen to his dreams. And if along the way she could say thank you to his "parents"—the Bingleys—and maybe find a Canadian doctor who might help her in her quest for a child, she would be satisfied.

Looking back now upon her arrival in Canada, she recalls her surprise to find so few people around, compared to Indian railway stations and airports.

Shyly she greeted Anand, who could not curb a twinkle in his warm brown eyes, obviously delighted to see her, but restraining his emotions in typical Indian fashion.

But Mrs. Bingley did not hesitate to engulf the little Indian woman, dressed in her colorful sari, in her arms, clucking over her like a mother hen. In the months ahead she took Sarla into her heart like the daughter she'd never had. Her strong personality and outgoing manner made up for Sarla's timorous nature, and an understanding between the two women developed, even though limited by language.

During his final year at Toronto Bible College, Anand and Sarla talked a great deal about their future. Dr. Boehmer was urging Anand to continue with his education, and even went so far as to contact several seminaries about enrollment and scholarships. Anand applied to Trinity Evangelical Divinity School in the United States and was accepted.

Letters from India brought other offers, including an urgent request from the Delhi Bible Institute that Anand return to teach there again.

In May 1969, however, just before graduation, Anand was studying to preach on a Tuesday evening on the call of Moses.

"As I was preparing," he recalls, "it seemed that the Lord was speaking to my heart—'now you go back to your own people.' And it came so forcefully that I couldn't resist it."

That very day Anand told Sarla, "The Lord is calling me back to India. We'll be going back; we're not going to the States."

It was harder telling the Bingleys who had been looking forward to having Anand and Sarla within visiting distance for another few years. Already in their eighties, they did not feel strong enough to visit Anand in India. But when they heard of Anand's call from God they assured him, "If the Lord is calling you, go back, and we'll stand with you."

Anand and Sarla spent three more months in Canada, while Anand served as pastor at the Leaside Bible Chapel, which had been his spiritual home all through the years in Toronto. The church promised to stand behind him when he returned to India, but did not make a regular financial commitment.

In October 1969, Anand and Sarla said good-bye to their many friends as they left for India. Sure of his call back to his motherland, Anand was nevertheless unsure of what God wanted him to do there. One thought kept nagging in his heart—God wants me in Rajasthan or Bihar—the two most spiritually desolate provinces in India.

What he would do, how he would work, where they would live, were all unresolved. God had said "India," and that's all Anand needed to know.

12

No Well to Draw From

The eastern province of Bihar, one of the poorest areas in India, had long beckoned Anand—four-fifths of the people of Bihar were illiterate, two-thirds wretchedly impoverished, over half were landless, and most were Hindu. Years back he had translated two stories about Bihar which had left a vivid impression of the desperate need of its people.

In the face of such hopelessness, what could one man do? Yet Anand was driven by an intense conviction that God had called him back to his own people, and that He would use him as a key to the locked hearts of Hindus whose blindness had been indelibly imprinted in his mind.

But terrible as the situation was in Bihar, Rajasthan—the second largest and most backward state in the nation—became Anand's specific burden.

Rajasthan was not consolidated until after independence in 1947. During the British rule 26 maharajahs reigned over their desert states by consent of the colonial power. These states served as a buffer zone against other anti-British factions. A total of 565 princes were allowed continued autonomy in their own fiefdoms throughout India.

The princes' prerogatives were secured by treaties with the British. In general, they maintained law and order in their areas, and relieved the colonial rulers from stretching themselves even further.

Lord Canning, the first viceroy, explained, "These patches of native government served as a breakwater to the storm which would otherwise have swept over us in one great wave."

Bizarre tales are told of the maharajahs. One received his weight in gold from his dutiful followers on his birthday. Another built lavish apartments equipped with telephones and air conditioning for his favorite dogs, who lived far better than most of his impoverished subjects.

The Maharajah of Bharatpur, who was renowned for his hunting, carpeted his apartments with wall-to-wall tiger skins and drove a silver-plated Rolls-Royce.

In Jaipur, the capital of Rajasthan, it was told that a fabulous treasure had been buried in the hills above the city guarded by a vigilant army of Rajputs. Each maharajah was allowed to visit the site once in his lifetime to select a piece of jewelry. One necklace is said to have had three tiers of rubies the size of pigeons' eggs, and three enormous emeralds, the largest of which weighed 90 carats.

Most of Rajasthan is a hostile desert, with blistering heat in the summer and biting cold winds in the winter. Camels replace the elephant as beast of burden in the arid landscape.

The historian Toynbee described Rajasthan as a "lean country ... sumptuous palaces have been wrung out of Rajasthan's skinny plains and bony mountains by the poor peasants .... Hard countries are apt to produce hardy people. Rajasthan is about as hard a country as there could be."

It has also been a hard country to penetrate with the Gospel. In granting the Rajahs political control, the British agreed not to interfere with the religious climate of their regions. Since these were generally strong Hindu leaders, they refused to allow missionaries to enter their territories. Only a few allowed even medical missionaries to come in and establish hospitals.

But when the "native states" were consolidated under the new Indian government in 1950, a few south Indian Christians entered cautiously. One mission, Operation Mobilization, sent numerous teams into the desert villages, finding time after time that the people had literally never heard the word "Jesus." Several Brethren Assemblies and Full Gospel churches were planted. The Scottish Presbyterians had come a hundred years earlier, and were now united with the Anglicans and Presbyterians to form the Church of North India (CNI).

Anand and Sarla had left Canada for India on October 16, 1969. In the four years he'd been away there had been great changes in his beloved homeland. Indira Gandhi had become prime minister two years earlier; the second India-Pakistan war fought over Kashmir had been won by India; and great strides were being heralded in agriculture, electrification, and education.

But less than 2000 Indian citizens admitted to more than $1300 a year taxable income, and more than 400 million were living on the knife-edge of starvation, spending less than two rupees (US 20 cents) a day.

To Anand, however, the spiritual poverty of his people, bound in idolatry and hopeless cycles of life and death, was the desperate need to which he could speak. He felt an indescribable sense of resting in God's hand, ready to be projected into the arena. A special power was waiting to be unleashed, and he had but to find the launching pad.

For three months after their arrival back in India, Anand and Sarla stayed in Jhansi with her parents. Mama and Papa Jacob had aged. Sarla's brother, Anil, had moved to Agra, and her sister, Kusum, was studying at South India Biblical Seminary. Both Rev. McKay and Russell Self were still there and joyfully welcomed Anand back to India, relieved that the haunting fear of his defection was laid to rest.

At the first opportunity Mama Jacob asked Sarla if she'd been able to find medical help for her childlessness.

But Sarla shook her head. "Anand said going to a doctor in Canada for such treatment is very expensive."

Sarla told her mother she'd also mentioned the subject to Mrs. Bingley, whose reaction came as a surprise to Sarla. "If God doesn't give you a child, you should accept it as His will. You shouldn't force your own way."

So Sarla dropped the subject—except with God. She continued to pray daily that the Lord would give her a child. And back in India her mother was praying with her.

But now her mother had some good news for Sarla. "In the mission hospital here there is a very sweet little baby, about eighteen months old. Her mother died in childbirth. Many people have wanted to adopt her—even one of the missionaries tried to get permission, but couldn't. I think they will give her to you. Tomorrow we should go and see her."

Initially Anand hadn't been interested in adoption. "An orphan is still a stigma in India," he explains. "I was afraid the child would always have a complex. So I wasn't too keen on the idea. But," he adds with a sparkle in his eyes, "when I saw Pinkie, I was immediately drawn to her."

He still keeps her baby picture, taken the day they brought her home from the hospital, on his desk.

And so it was that Pinkie, whose real name is Pushbanjali, after the aunt she never met, came into Anand and Sarla's life, to become the joy of their home, the delight of their hearts—and the answer to many years of prayer.

Even during those exciting first days of being parents, Anand continued to spend hours in meditation and prayer, seeking direction for their future.

Before he'd gone to Canada, he'd visited Brethren Assembly workers all over north India. He'd met M. A. Thomas in Kota, Rajasthan, who had started an education program there. In fact, Anand had raised funds in Canada for Thomas' ministry. Now he wrote him asking about prospects for ministry in Rajasthan. Thomas wrote back, encouraging Anand to come to Kota and see for himself.

This seemed to be the final indication that they should go to Rajasthan. In 1970, Anand and Sarla moved to the town of Kota to serve God in this dry and dusty region, one of the most spiritually barren areas of the world. One-tenth of one percent of the people would claim to be Christian; that is fifteen out of every ten thousand people, and the vast majority of these were only nominal Christians. Anand learned there were perhaps thirty small, struggling churches for a population of over thirty million.

Almost immediately after his arrival, Anand began preparing broadcasts for FEBA (Far Eastern Broadcasting Association), and letters began pouring in. Correspondence from his spiritually starving listeners came from towns and villages all over north India—people who had no other Gospel witness, no church, no pastor, no Christian neighbors, no Bibles nor literature.

It was urgent to get some kind of regular teaching to these Hindu listeners, who were searching as he had been not so many years ago.

Anand used a printed correspondence course based on the Gospel of John and placed a small ad in the local newspaper. Hundreds of people responded. In order to keep current with follow-up, he invited Arvind, Sarla's brother, who'd been correcting correspondence courses in Jhansi, to come and help him. Anand and Arvind spent their evenings responding to letters and correcting courses.

The radio time and courses were free; the postage was not. Though his Canadian friends had made no financial promises, their gifts always seemed to meet the needs of the moment, and Anand was confident God would continue to provide as long as he was obediently doing His work.

But there were problems. When their Sikh landlord discovered what Anand was doing he evicted them, and Anand's family had to search for other quarters.

During these months in Kota, Anand traveled from town to town, trying to evaluate what was being done and what would work best to begin to build the Church throughout Rajasthan.

"I came to the conclusion that we must have a very comprehensive, God-based program, including evangelism, follow-up, Bible training, and planting of churches," he explained later.

For a time Anand thought he could team up with M. A. Thomas in the work in Kota. But it soon became evident that their approach was different. Anand's vision for a broad outreach through Rajasthan was crystallizing. And the use of Hindi, declared one of the official languages of India in 1959, and the primary language for 300 million people in northern India, was of highest priority.

Sarla found this one of the most fulfilling times of her life, as she cared for her daughter and tried to keep the home running smoothly for her intensely-motivated husband. Many visitors dropped into the Chaudhari home, and Sarla never complained, though it was sometimes difficult to stretch the funds Anand could give her for food. She recalls at one stage they sold old newspapers to augment the gifts which came from Canada.

Anand realized the strain the demands of visitors and home made on Sarla, and he began looking for a young houseboy who could help her out. Just the simple act of grocery shopping was so much more difficult here than in Canada, since there was no refrigeration, and food had to be purchased at a variety of markets and stalls daily. Anand felt certain they could stretch their budget just a little more and began asking around for a reliable young boy to work for them.

Then one day Mohammed appeared at their door, saying he'd learned they were looking for a houseboy. He looked young for his twelve years, but there was a bright sparkle in his eyes, and Anand was strangely drawn to him. He learned that Mohammed came from a very poor Muslim family; he'd had to drop out of school because his parents needed him to work.

Within a short time Anand realized that Mohammed was indeed intelligent, quick to learn and interested in everything around him.

When Sarla taught in their first Vacation Bible School for the children in the area, Mohammed won most of the prizes.

Anand could not bear to see this gifted young mind wasted, so he paid school fees for Mohammed to attend the local school. Mohammed's mother, a devout Muslim, wasn't happy about the influence he was receiving and warned him, "Don't listen to that Christian talk." But she was grateful that Mohammed could work, and even go to school, and allowed him to stay on.

Since his return from studying in Canada, Anand received many invitations to speak in other parts of India. But when he read the invitation from the Brethren Assembly in Bombay, his heart raced.

He had not been back to Bombay since that day in 1954 when he had walked out of his aunt's house a pauper. He had written several letters, but his aunt and uncle had never answered.

But now he found himself in the city where he had made so many life-changing decisions. As he drove past the university, it brought back memories of agitated cell meetings, of his social awakening, of Joseph.

The ocean, rolling in never-ending splendour, brought him back to that moment on the beach when Christ's presence filled his life.

Even as he spoke in the conference, his mind churned with indecision. He wanted so much to see his aunt and uncle again. Perhaps they had mellowed over the years and would hear him out.

But another voice urged him not to go. As legal heir of his uncle's property, his visit could be misconstrued by the rest of the family. Was he trying to reestablish his claim after all these years?

Certainly his lack of income and property would be proof enough that his God had cut him short. Yet, he was well-educated and had traveled overseas, which gave him prestige and respect.

For days Anand struggled with the decision. And then on the last day of the conference, he hailed a taxi and instructed the driver to take him to Malabar Hill.

It seemed so natural to be driving up the winding road which overlooked the ocean below. The neighborhood had deteriorated in the seventeen years since he'd left, but though shops and other buildings crowded the once open spaces, he recognized many of the gracious homes of the wealthy.

Anand stopped the taxi before he reached the gate of the villa, and he told the driver to wait. He threw back his shoulders and pushed open the gate. As he started up the familiar path an elderly watchman sitting on his haunches under a shade tree hoisted himself stiffly to his feet.

Anand asked in Marathi, "Are Mr. and Mrs. Chaudhari in?" Even though he hadn't used the language in almost two decades, it came easily to his tongue.

The watchman seemed confused and shook his head. "Mr. Chaudhari's dead. But his wife's at home."

Taken aback, Anand reminded himself that he shouldn't be surprised. Seventeen years was a long time, and much had happened to him since last he'd stood here.

"So Auntie is alone," he thought. And there had been no son to perform the funeral rituals. And no one to speak a word of hope and eternal joy.

He wanted to know more—how had he died? How long has it been? Now he was more eager than ever to speak with his aunt face to face. Anand was tempted to walk up the familiar path to the door, but thought better of it. "Please tell her that her son, Anand, is here and would like to see her."

Perplexed, the watchman pulled his grubby dhoti tighter around his waist and hobbled up the path. Anand could see him disappear around the back of the house to pass his message on to the servant.

Anand felt his heart pounding in his chest as he stood at the gate for what seemed like hours. The news that his uncle was dead opened the wounds afresh, for he realized that he could never tell him about Christ again.

But perhaps his death had softened Auntie's heart. Perhaps she would be willing to see him now.

As the old man came hobbling around the corner of the house, Anand could tell nothing from his gnarled countenance.

But as he neared the gate, he shook his head, "Mrs. Chaudhari said to tell you, if you're still a Christian, she won't see you. She said as far as she's concerned, you're dead."

The old man looked at him expectantly, waiting for some kind of explanation for this strange interchange. But Anand couldn't say a word. He stared back for a moment as the finality of the words sank in, and then slowly turned to go back to his cab. Glancing once more at the home where he'd so long been the honored son, he saw the front door open and his aunt step out onto the veranda. For a moment their eyes met, and he saw the pain of loss. He was tempted to turn back and go to her, but before he could do so, she turned and disappeared into the house.

All the way on the long hot train ride back to Kota, Anand struggled with his deep sense of loss. His heart longed to see others come to Christ, but no one more than his auntie, who was the only blood tie he had left.

Back in Kota, Anand made preparations to move his family to Jaipur. In the torrid August heat the family moved to the Pink City.

At first Mohammed's mother and father refused to allow him to go along, but he protested so vehemently that in the end they relented. However, they agreed only on condition that Anand also take his younger brother along to Jaipur and send both boys to school there.

So by the time the Anand Chaudhari family arrived in Jaipur they had grown to six.

Jaipur was founded more than 250 years ago by Maharaja Sawai Jai Singh, a poet and philosopher king, who was considered one of the world's greatest astronomers. He translated Euclid's Principles of Geometry into Sanskrit, and built an outdoor observatory of stair-cases and massive masonry instruments which still accurately measure the movements of the sun and earth.

Today Jaipur is a bustling city of commerce and craft. Jai Singh invited traders and artisans from all over India to settle in his city, and it still has a booming export market in jewelry, semi-precious stones, handicrafts, fabrics, pottery, and brassware. But, the old city still exudes a quaint architectural atmosphere of pink lattice-work palaces and the proud fort.

However, by the time the Chaudhari's moved into Jaipur, more than half a million people had spilled out of the original city walls into modern Jaipur. Thousands who lived in huts of cardboard, thatch and scraps, bathed on the street corners at public taps. Squatters had settled wherever they could among the more substantial Eastern-style homes.

On the busy roads nasty-tempered camels, their burdens perched as lightly as fleas on their backs, arrogantly ignored the confusion around them. They moved insolently through the crush of rickshaws, pedicabs, bicycles, wagons, carts, dilapidated buses bulging with people, trucks and cars. Every vehicle that had a horn used it.

There were thousands of Muslims and Sikhs in Jaipur, and the city was dotted with Hindu temples and flower-bedecked shrines.

But there was little Christian influence in this city of more than a half million people. There were only three tiny churches serving an ingrown Christian community.

Several of the early mission churches, including the Scottish Presbyterians, had united to form the Church of North India, and there were two small CNI churches in Jaipur which had a limited outreach beyond their doors.

The Scottish Presbyterians had established a high school almost one hundred years earlier, but with the departure of the last mission-aries in the fifties, the school was in disrepair and ready to close for lack of funds.

Anand and Sarla soon found a house to rent on the Church of North India mission compound. Now, after eleven years of prepara-tion, experience, and dreaming dreams, Anand felt he was at last ready to begin the work that God had called him to when he spoke with Him on that lonely beach in Bombay.

In Anand's methodical mind, his work was laid out clearly. The goal was before him—to bring light to the 30 million people of Rajasthan who'd lived in Hindu darkness for so long. No matter that his own people had rejected the message; nor that he was alone, without property, funds or institution behind him. God had called him to help raise the church in north India, and Jaipur was his launching pad.

The responsibilities he'd had in Kota continued. He prepared the weekly broadcasts over FEBA, and made regular trips to Delhi to record the programs. Letters continued to pour in to the new address, and the correspondence school rolls grew.

So far the funds coming from friends in Canada met their simple needs. The Leaside Bible Chapel and several other small churches sent gifts faithfully, and the Bingleys remained true to their promise to stand with him.

But Anand knew that when God began planting His Church in this arid desert, the struggling flocks would have to have trained shep-herds who knew how to feed them the Bread of Life and the Living Water. And as far as he knew, there was no Hindi seminary training such leaders.

That was goal number one—and Anand wasted little time in getting started. His first step was to form a board of Christian leaders—pastors and businessmen—so that the Rajasthan Bible Institute could be registered with the government.

The beginning of 1973 saw four young men living in the Chaudhari home, as Anand began teaching a one-year Bible course.

By now Pushbanjali was a delightful five year old who had wrapped herself around her father's heart. No one could light up his eyes or lift his tired spirit like her childish prattle.

He recalls how she made friends with a family who was to become a very important part of their lives. There were a number of dogs on the mission compound. Dogs, like children, like company. Anand noticed a little Pomeranian had a knack for running away from home to frolic with their dog. A little girl, a few years older than Pinkie, would come and get her pet. Ramona Alexander and Pinkie soon became fast friends.

Then one day a bright-eyed young girl appeared at the door, shyly asking for "Uncle Chaudhari."

She introduced herself as Regina Alexander, Ramona's older sister. Her eyes lit up when she entered the room and her shyness melted as she saw a large bookcase of books. Her purpose became clear—she'd learned of the books through her sister, and wondered if Uncle Chaudhari would allow her to borrow one.

The friendship between the Alexanders and the Chaudharis grew, and soon Regina's mother began coming to Bible class held in Anand's home. Years later, after Regina finished Bible school, she became Anand's assistant in the office.

Anand could have used such help just then, for opportunities were developing at a faster pace than he had imagined. The four young men were avid students with whom he tried to spend as much time as possible. He had already learned that discipling is the best form of teaching, and he gave his students every opportunity to watch him live what he taught.

FEBA asked Anand to prepare a second weekly radio broadcast, this one for thirty minutes. The responses mushroomed, so that Anand almost hated to go the mailbox. It was becoming impossible for the small crew of students and Anand to keep up with answering letters and marking lessons.

It had become obvious that the next step was to open the Rajasthan Bible Institute officially as a full-time school, and for that he needed more space.

And he needed money. Anand new that the friends in Canada were giving sacrificially, and they could not increase their donations enough to build a school and pay for the increasing costs of courses, transportation and staff. The Bingleys were no longer working, and their resources were limited.

And the church in Rajasthan—the tiny, sleeping church, was the proverbial drop in the bucket when it came to the needs of northern India.

Anand had experienced God's care in miraculous ways before. But the provisions had always been for himself and his immediate family. Did he have the audacity to ask God to provide funds for property, staff, and other expenses that would run into literally thousands and thousands of dollars? Who besides the few churches in the Toronto area knew him well enough to trust him with such large sums? He was not a fund raiser; in fact, he found it very difficult to present his financial needs to anyone.

But there was no question in his mind that God has placed him in Jaipur to begin the Rajasthan Bible Institute and to develop evangelists and church planters. As he poured over his beloved Scriptures, the plan crystallized in his mind. The experimental year with the students proved it could work; the response to the radio messages evidenced the deep spiritual hunger of his people in darkness.

A simple thing like money shouldn't stand in the way of God's program, but, humanly speaking, he saw no possibilities to gain funds.

Then in August 1974, Anand received a letter from the Bingleys asking him to come to Canada. "We are getting older and may not be here much longer. We want to see you once more. We'll take care of your tickets and you can stay with us while you're in Canada."

Once more Anand left Sarla behind, this time for only three months. He didn't know how God was going to open the conduits to the funds they needed in Rajasthan.

He only knew that his mother's last words were still ringing in his ears: "Anand, don't hold your hand out to strangers." If there was going to be a Bible school in Rajasthan, God would have to provide the money in His own way.

So determined was he to let God provide that Anand "closed up shop" before he left Jaipur. He paid off all the workers with the understanding that there would be a completely new beginning when he returned, but only if God clearly directed and supplied the necessary funds.

13

Too Big for His Boots?

Sometimes Anand must have had moments of doubt about starting his own ministry. There were plenty of opportunities for him to serve the Lord in India without stepping out on a limb alone. The Delhi area, which headquartered several dozen Western mission agencies, was crying for more evangelists, teachers, and pastors. Wouldn't it be easier to join up with one of those groups, have someone else worry about the funds, and get on with the job?

In fact, Rev. Duff pled with Anand to return to Delhi Bible Institute. But though an impressive building had been constructed while Anand was away, the school could not cater to students who spoke only Hindi.

Anand decided he could not return to the same frustrations he'd left four years earlier. He was sure that God had brought him back to India for a broader work. "My calling was definite," he reiterates, "to use mass media to reach Hindi-speaking people."

Many times he searched his own heart to ask if there were some reason why he could not fit into the missionaries' program. Did this independence stem from sin in his own heart? Didn't the Holy Spirit give direction to them too? Didn't their purposes agree with his, to see Hindus come to Christ?

But he was constantly reminded of the masses in northern India, totally untouched by the church, who saw Christianity as a Western intrusion, completely out of the realm of reality for them. The fact that the Christian message had come primarily from Europeans intensified their feelings that it was non-Indian.

Anand knew differently. His burning desire was to pry open the hearts of his Hindu people to demonstrate that one of them, an Indian, a former Brahmin—one who loved his country and its people, who could speak its languages and think philosophically with them—could also be totally Christian.

Whenever he grappled with this question, he came back to the honest realization that he was not seeking for a kingdom, or power. But he had a gut feeling about what would cut through the traditional barriers, and he was convinced he had to do it the way God had shown him. His board encouraged him all the way, but as individuals they had limited funds to offer.

Logically, it was inconceivable that Anand should even think about purchasing property. Jaipur was growing faster than the city could cope, and property was either nonexistent, exhorbitantly expensive, or enmeshed in legal and traditional regulations that made it impossible to obtain.

But there was a small section of the CNI mission which had never been built upon, and since it was already allocated for church work, it should be easy to obtain permission.

However, when Anand went to the officers of the trust, he learned the piece would cost more than $75,000—about five times what he'd been willing to offer. It was far too small for the work he had in mind. And he didn't have enough money to offer even a token down payment.

He'd hoped that he would have the promise of property before he left for Canada, but that was not to be.

Even the reunion with the Bingleys could not erase the dejection he felt. He had returned to India in 1969 with such high hopes and plans for evangelizing north India, but he felt that nothing of substance had been accomplished during the past five years.

"I had ideas and plans—but nothing was happening. I felt spiritually dry and powerless. I wasn't even able to preach," he recalls. His audiences in Canada listened unenthusiastically to the vision he presented.

One night shortly after he arrived at the Bingleys', the sense of disappointment and failure overwhelmed him. Alone in his room he fell on his knees with his open Bible before him, beseeching God for His touch.

"Lord, if you're not with me, I'm packing up and leaving on the first flight to India," he groaned, as he prostrated himself on the floor. "Give me back your power."

Anand broke down weeping before the Lord, baring his heart, pleading and praying, "Lord, this is your work, your vision, your call. I am only a servant."

Exhausted, he lay back on his bed, but the anguish of his heart did not let him rest. So he was once again on his knees, weeping and pleading with the Lord to confirm His call.

Sometime during the night Mr. Bingley heard a noise and came to Anand's room to investigate. As he opened the door he was startled to hear Anand's urgently-pleading voice, but he could not understand a word he was saying. As his eyes grew accustomed to the dark, he could see Anand's form prostrate on the floor.

Quietly he closed the door so as not to disturb him.

In the morning Mr. Bingley tried to find out from Anand what had been going on. "I don't know what awakened me, but at about three or four in the morning I heard a noise and came to your room to see what was happening. I saw you on your knees, and heard you talking, but I couldn't understand what you were saying."

Then he added words which both thrilled and chilled Anand's heart. "I felt a presence in the room that I couldn't explain. So I just left without disturbing you."

Anand couldn't explain what happened either. All he knew was that he fell asleep on the floor, and awoke feeling refreshed and renewed. The dryness had gone; he felt a tremendous sense of God's presence.

Shortly after that he was asked to speak at the Ontario Bible College convocation. Instead of dryness and discouragement, he felt an inexplicable joy and freedom. He found himself spilling out his dreams with power and conviction—the Bible school, the radio work and its growing follow-up, the correspondence courses, and the churches to be planted in the spiritual desert of Rajasthan.

Young men knew about dreaming dreams, and he could see excitement in the eyes of the students as he shared his vision. But it was an elderly mission statesman, Dr. Boehmer, who took him aside after the meeting to offer practical advice.

"You've got some mighty big plans there, young man—and they're going to take a lot of money. Where are you going to get it?"

When Anand admitted that he had no source for funds outside of the few small Bible chapels in Toronto and the personal generosity of the Bingleys, Dr. Boehmer thought for a moment.

"I think I should talk with Dr. Percy. He can put you in touch with George Doxsee, the Canadian president of *Christian Nationals*. They often help projects like this."

So it was that one evening Anand found himself in Dr. Doxsee's home to learn about an organization he'd never heard of before, the Christian Nationals Evangelism Commission. He learned of an undreamed resource to help launch his vision.

After he'd explained something of his background and his dreams, he could see Dr. Doxsee's excitement and interest building. But he also asked insightful questions that surprised Anand. He seemed to understand why he was going out on his own instead of fitting into existing programs. He asked a lot about his board—what kind of people they were, what responsibilities they assumed, what churches they represented.

At one point Dr. Doxsee asked, "Are you getting any support for this work from India?"

Regretfully, Anand had to respond that he'd not asked any of the tiny local churches to help with the expenses, that he'd pretty well managed with the gifts that had come from Canada.

"Don't you think Indian Christians should share in the costs of evangelizing their own people?" he was asked.

Even as Anand explained the extreme poverty of most of the Christians, and the lack of cooperation he had seen between denominations in India, he had to admit this was an area he could explore more. Yet with dismay he realized that no school would ever be built in Rajasthan by the weak and poverty-stricken church there. Why, a pastor was fortunate to receive $30 or $40 a month from his church, hardly enough to keep his large family of children fed and clothed.

But then the conversation took a different turn, and Anand discovered that this man was sincerely interested in helping him. As Dr. Doxsee explained:

"Christian Nationals has been helping national ministries like yours since 1943. We wouldn't get involved in running your work. Your board would have to make all the decisions. But we would expect regular reports and financial statements so we can tell our supporters what's going on."

Before the evening was out, it was arranged that Dr. Doxsee would visit Jaipur on his forthcoming trip to India, to meet with the board and see the work firsthand. In the meantime, Anand would proceed with filling out applications and getting recommendations.

"*Christian Nationals* doesn't have a big pot of money somewhere, Anand," Dr. Doxsee warned before they parted. "We'll have to find people interested in helping your work before we can make a regular commitment. But I have a feeling God is in this, and there shouldn't be any trouble raising funds."

With this exciting possibility and the promise from Leaside Chapel, and a few other friends, that they would try to help him purchase property, Anand returned to India with high hopes.

Even before his return, God was moving in Jaipur. During the Sunday school Christmas celebration a man came up to Sarla to ask about Anand's need for property.

"There's a piece of land on the national highway that's for sale. I think it would be large enough for a school. Your husband ought to look into it."

In the excitement of having Anand home again, Sarla forgot all about this news, until one noon when they were sitting at lunch discussing the school.

"Oh, I forgot to tell you that a man at the Christmas party told me about some property over on the national road that's for sale. It may be gone by now because that was about three weeks ago."

When he saw the property, Anand's heart leapt with excitement. It had been the home of one of the maharajah's favorite dancers, but the substantial house had fallen into disrepair. There were also several smaller outbuildings and stables at the back of the property which could be remodeled. The piece was at least four times as large as the mission property they'd been considering.

But the excitement was soon dashed when he learned that the property had been sold to a real estate man who had already given a large down payment. He would be closing the deal at the end of January.

However, the owner promised that if for any reason the deal fell through, Anand could have first option.

During the next two weeks students, board members and friends spent hours in prayer for the property. Anand had that special conviction that he'd had before, that the property would be theirs. So it was no surprise to him when the owner, Mr. Hine, came to him early in February with the news that the real estate man had failed to raise the money.

Without hesitation, Anand responded that he'd take it. Even he smiles at his audacity now. "I promised him that I would pay the full amount by the end of August. We didn't have any money at all at that time."

But Anand had walked with God long enough to have confidence He could provide for him, even when there were no visible means to do so.

Again the Lord moved through his Canadian friends, who raised all but $5000 for the purchase of "Mubarak Bagh"(Blessed Garden). When Dr. Doxsee visited Jaipur early in 1975 and saw the property, he agreed to try to raise the balance through CNEC.

He assured Anand that he would recommend to the international headquarters of *Christian Nationals* in San Jose, California, that Rajasthan Bible Institute and its affiliated ministries be accepted into the fellowship of CNEC. It was agreed that they would start by supporting six evangelist/students at $50 a month, which would enable Anand to open the school as soon as they moved into the property.

In June 1975, Rajasthan Bible Institute opened with six new students on the recently acquired RBI campus. "Campus" was perhaps exaggerated. The young men moved their few possessions into a small room in the house while repair work was going on.

Anand had handpicked these six men whom he hoped to train to become the teachers and leaders of the work in the future. He had been able to make arrangements for them to write their exams under the prestigious, though liberal-oriented Serampore College, which would grant a B.Th. upon successful completion of the courses. The syllabus and texts were prescribed by Serampore, but Anand taught most of the classes, giving the men a solid Biblical foundation.

Some, like Arvind, one of Sarla's brothers, and Mohammed, had been with the Chaudharis for a number of years, helping with correspondence courses and in other ares of ministry. Anand believed they had leadership qualities as well as Christian commitment.

Mohammed had already caused him the heartache of a son. After finishing high school, he'd returned to Kota to work, and Anand heard disturbing reports of his spiritual condition. But one day a penitent Mohammed stood at his door, pleading to be taken back. He'd watched the cremation of a Hindu friend, and the flames shooting in the air reminded him of the "fire of hell." In spite of the wrath and threats of his parents, Mohammed returned to Jaipur to continue his studies, this time to serve God and not just to benefit himself.

Leslie had been a young convert when Anand worked in Delhi. He completed his B.A. at an agricultural university, but felt God's call to Christian work, and was eager to come to RBI to study.

Dalip met the Chaudharis in 1974 while he was working for Pan American Airways in Jaipur. As a young Christian, he sought out Christian fellowship, and ended up staying with Anand for several weeks.

Nand had been serving in Lucknow with Operation Mobilization when Anand first met him. Nand had grown up in a nominal Christian home and met Christ while working for a Christian organization. But now he was a fired-up evangelist who was drawn by Anand's vision, and spent time with the Chaudharis whenever he could get to Jaipur.

Jeral had been a typist at the Delhi Bible Institute when Anand had worked there. Though he was just a nominal Christian he showed promise, and when he came to Anand later to ask to work with him, Anand agreed, hoping to harness his gifts to glorify God.

"I wanted these young men to grow with a vision and burden for the whole of north India, not just for Rajasthan—but for all of Hindi-speaking India."

So day by day, Anand built into these young men the vision God had given him. He challenged them with excellence, since they were required to meet the high academic standards of Serampore.

"I taught them most of the subjects from the first year to the last—all five years. At the same time they helped in the follow-up work. We had about 8000 in the correspondence courses at the time as a result of the two weekly radio broadcasts," Anand recollects.

The five-hour bus trips to Delhi to record the programs were beginning to wear on Anand, and he and the board began to pray about the possibility of erecting a recording studio right on the RBI grounds.

In fact, some time during 1975 Anand received a letter from a former Toronto Bible College student, Fred Simmonds, then working with Trans World Radio. TWR was building a new station in Sri Lanka and would be looking for Hindi programs in the near future. So it seemed the radio opportunities would be expanding—all the more need for a studio. But of course that was out of the question now.

Besides teaching and preparing the six students for their Bachelor of Theology exams, at the same time Anand was keeping one step ahead of them by doing the Bachelors of Divinity program himself through Serampore.

In the fall of 1977 Anand had just come back from another trip overseas, this time under the auspices of *Christian Nationals* where he'd been able to present the ministry of the Rajasthan Bible Institute to a wider audience of Christians in the United States.

A generous gift for radio equipment was encouraging, but without a studio building, it did not relieve him of the wearisome trips to Delhi.

However, late in 1977 TWR once again approached Anand and offered to build a studio on the RBI campus.

But nagging at him was the sense that God wasn't fulfilling his vision yet. Anand complained, "At the end of 1977 I was feeling discouraged. We were busy; the students were coming along well; the studio was going up; the response from the radio programs encouraging. But we were not having an impact on the whole of Rajasthan— and that was my burden."

Anand had always been fascinated by maps, and once again he pulled out his detailed maps of Rajasthan, noting the widely scattered areas where correspondence students lived.

He'd been studying in the book of Acts and was reminded of the tremendous impact of Peter and the other apostles upon the city of Jerusalem. The high priest had accused this small handful of men in Acts 5:8 stating, "You have filled Jerusalem with your teaching."

It was as though God were saying, "If Peter could do it, you can do it."

As he poured over the maps, suddenly, a clear pattern stood out; there were people who'd responded to his radio broadcast in every one of the larger towns of Rajasthan—people who wanted to know more about the Lord Jesus and who wanted to study the Bible through correspondence courses.

Could these towns be saturated with literature and house-to-house visitation, and new contacts made for the Gospel?

Anand secured the most recent census reports from a government office and began listing the Rajasthan towns of 10,000 to 100,000 population. There were 157 of them.

Pondering the maps and praying for wisdom, Anand spent hours secluded in his study as God's plan begin to take shape. He would organize teams of evangelists to visit the 157 towns—78 this year; 79

next. Townspeople had an advantage over the village folk who lived in 30,000 tiny villages all over Rajasthan.

Townspeople tended to be literate, and were the center for social life and prestige for the neighboring villages. Most townspeople had relations in the villages, so the influence would filter down to them. And the people in the larger towns were far less suspicious of and resistant to strangers.

The plan seemed perfect, but it would take a lot of money to support such a large team and purchase literature.

For three months Anand and the students prayed about the new project. Did he dare go to his new backers with this almost outrageous request for funds?

Once again he looked over the figures he'd tried to draw up conservatively.

A reasonable allowance for an evangelist working in the villages would be about $35 a month. For thirty-two evangelists that would come to about $1100, plus transportation, accommodations and literature.

Literature alone would come to a mind-boggling US $45,000 for the first eight months of the project.

Yet, the more Anand and his team thought about the project, the more sense it made. In every town there were correspondence course students who had indicated an interest in becoming Christians— lonely and without any other spiritual fellowship. In many towns there were radio listeners who had written in saying they were secret believers—yet there was not a single church to which they could send them.

If the evangelists covered each of these towns with literature packets, visited the secret believers, held open-air meetings, and offered correspondence courses, surely a nucleus of believers would emerge. And Rajasthan would begin to have a Christian witness.

Week after week Anand and his team prayed, asking God for some indication that He was behind the project; something to give them assurance they could provide for the families of the thirty-two evangelists they would have to recruit; some indication that they could place the first order for literature.

Then in February 1978, at the annual board meeting, Anand placed the project before his board members.

Their response was predictable. "Where are you going to get the money for such a program? You need funds for more staff to correct correspondence courses and do radio follow-up. You need more buildings for the school. The idea is wonderful, but we don't have the money."

Back and forth the arguments ranged—as the board recognized the careful planning and committed goals of this intensive evange-lism campaign, yet realistically shook their heads over the unrealistic costs. Literature alone would run between sixty and seventy thou-sands rupees a month (six to seven thousand dollars). And RBI's monthly budget at that time was only a little over three hundred dollars.

During one of the breaks in the day-long meeting, Anand took a few minutes to check his mail. Seeing a letter from Allen Finley, international president of *Christian Nationals,* he opened it. Once again God had revealed His will just when Anand needed to have an answer. He took the letter back to the board.

"Greetings in Christ. We have received a special gift of $2000 from Mr. _____ of Michigan . . . . Do you have some vital special project which we could report to this donor?"

The board responded as Anand knew they would. The money was far from what they needed for Project 78 and 79, but when God placed a down payment, He never reneged on the balance.

And so Anand was instructed to inform Allen Finley of the province-wide vision God had given them. Anand wrote, "There are 157 towns (10,000 to 100,000 people) in Rajasthan. We have corres-pondence course students and listeners in each town. They need to be visited and counseled. As we were thinking about this we felt the need of intensive evangelism in each town of our province. We thought about this and decided to visit 78 towns this year and 79 towns next year. That's why we have called this effort Project 78 and 79."

The curtains were about to open on Act One for the church in Rajasthan.

14

The Pressures Mount

The hardest part was waiting for news from the eight teams out in the towns. Once they finally left the RBI campus everything seemed to quiet down.

The first six months of 1978 had been bedlam. The much-needed studio built by TWR was dedicated in January. Now it would be easier to produce the seven weekly programs based on Dr. J. Vernon McGee's studies of the Bible. Twenty-four evangelists for the teams were hired; 100,000 pieces of literature ordered.

Anand had helped to prepare a special booklet for Hindu women to be included in the literature packet, since there had been nothing written in Hindi dealing with the unique problems of Indian women.

The eight teams had been sent out to carefully selected towns across central Rajasthan—towns large enough to ensure that many of the people could read; populous enough so that strangers wouldn't be spotted the minute they entered, as they would be in a village.

The evangelists had applied to take part in the campaign in response to invitations by word of mouth and correspondence. Most of them had been involved in some kind of evangelism ministry, primarily Operation Mobilization teams, and knew what was ahead of them. Being part of an evangelistic team meant leaving their wives and children behind in their home villages for months on end, and surviving on a minimum stipend of about $35 a month.

But there had been no lack of eager volunteers, and Anand's heart was moved as he recognized their spirit of compassion for their people, and their willingness to trust God for their protection and their families' needs. They all knew that scorn, rejection, and even danger awaited them in those vast Christless regions, especially with the growing antagonism of militant Hindu groups.

Telephone contact was virtually unheard of between these smaller towns and Jaipur; and writing reports in the "heat of battle" was difficult, especially for those unaccustomed to putting their thoughts on paper.

So Anand and his staff waited for the first report.

God was putting all the pieces together once again. The first gift of $2000 through friends of *Christian Nationals* had been followed up by others—some large, some small—but enough to enable Anand to place a large order for literature that would keep the teams supplied at least for a month.

Early in 1978 Regina Alexander joined the RBI staff, having completed her course at the Union Biblical Seminary in Yoetemal. Her gift of organization filled Anand's need for someone to keep all the details in order.

Regina, herself, was excited to be able to help in the ministry she'd seen grow up with her. "Uncle Chaudhari is a special father to me," she explains. "You can see compassion and love in his eyes—that impression has never gone since I've known him as a little girl."

Meanwhile, while the radio and correspondence follow-up kept students and staff busy at RBI, the teams were methodically covering their assigned towns.

When the reports started filtering back, it was clear the evangelists found themselves in enemy territory.

In Bharatapur, known for its tiger hunts in the days of the British Raj, Robin Masih and the other evangelists reported they had decided to split up to cover the sprawling town as rapidly as possible. The general idea in this first "blitz" was to quickly visit every home with a literature packet, inviting people to write in for a free correspondence course. Hopefully the evangelists would get in and out before the anti-Christian groups could organize their opposition.

Wherever Robin and his co-workers stopped to give out literature, a small crowd of curiosity seekers gathered to listen and stare. They were soon surrounded by women carrying water on their heads, sweat-drenched laborers glad for any excuse to rest their burdens, beggars, bright-eyed students, little girls carrying their runny-nosed baby brothers on their hips, and often a Hindu priest.

The very first day two team members, Gopal and Sundar, found themselves surrounded by such a crowd. And as they explained the story of Jesus Christ, angry voices broke in, deriding them. "Go back where you came from. We don't want your foreign religion here."

Others turned to the crowd shouting, "Don't listen to these agents of Westerners. They're trying to convert our people."

Finally one of the men grabbed Gopal's bag of literature. As he pulled back, another shoved him over. Several jumped on the two evangelists, beating them with their fists and shouting, "Get out of here; we don't want you Christians in our town." In the fracas, the book bags fell to the ground, and were dumped out—the precious papers flying away in the wind, or crushed in the dirt. A gang of rowdy fellows, who'd joined in just for the fun, began picking up the booklets and ripping them apart—even the shoulder bags were destroyed.

Gopal and Sundar picked themselves up gingerly from the dirt, and vainly tried to gather the few packets that had escaped destruction.

But the young bullies in the crowd had tasted blood, and began threatening the evangelists with sticks. Realizing they were out-numbered, Gopal and Sundar turned and ran down the street and back to the team's rented room.

That night the team members comforted each other, praying for courage to face the angry townspeople another day. The next morn-ing the two teams decided to work together, feeling there was safety in numbers.

But the same gang of ruffians was waiting for them, lounging outside the little shops which lined the narrow dirt streets.

Without warning the gang moved in on the team, surrounding it, and once again pushed and shoved until they got the book bags off their shoulders. And again the evangelists saw their precious litera-ture ripped to shreds and crumpled in the mud.

After this defeat, Robin suggested that they seek out the radio contacts who lived in the town.

What a contrast! Their listeners, some of whom were secret believ-ers, welcomed and encouraged the team and gave them suggestions as to where to start distributing literature, so that eventually all of Bharatapur's homes were touched.

One of the prime purposes of Project 78 and 79 was to make contact with the people in every town who had responded to a radio program or were enrolled in the correspondence course. A survey had shown there was at least one, and usually a group of several, who had written in from most towns in Rajasthan.

But no one was more surprised than Daniel Masih and his team to find a group of young boys in the town of Hindaun, meeting together in a rented room to read the Bible and pray. The boys were between eleven and sixteen years old. They had seen some of the team members passing out literature and had greeted them eagerly, inviting them to come to a little room behind a shop.

These boys had listened to Anand's radio broadcast, and as a result enrolled in the correspondence course. Upon completion of the course, each boy received a New Testament from RBI, and they began studying and praying together.

Daniel could hardly believe his ears as the students eagerly plied the team with questions about the Bible.

"How did you get this room?" he asked.

"We collect a few rupees from each one and rent it from the owner," was the reply.

What made this even more amazing is that there wasn't another Christian, a church, or evangelist in the town.

Later, when Project 78 and 79 was completed, Daniel Masih and his family moved to Hindaun so he could work more closely with these young men.

Most of the people in Hindaun are Jains, a sect which grew out of Hinduism and emphasizes such an utter respect for all forms of life that a true Jain will strain every drop of water, and wear a veil over his or her mouth to avoid inhaling insects.

Jains do not consider themselves Hindus, but there's a fierce loyalty to everything Indian, and deep anger when a Hindu converts to Christianity.

But the most militant Hindu force in the country is the Rastriya Swayam Sevak Sangh (RSS), and Hindaun boasted a large chapter.

As Daniel witnessed from house to house, sharing the precious name of Jesus, he found many hungry for truth and ready to listen. But if he returned to the same place several times, RSS agents would warn the family not to invite him into the house. Most people were too afraid of the consequences to defy their threats.

One night as Daniel walked home after a long day of visitation, a gang of RSS men apprehended him. Surrounding him, they forced him to go with them to a Hindu rally. The whole night through he was held prisoner and was forced to listen to speeches denouncing Christians and others who tried to convert Hindus. He realized they were fiercely zealous and determined to stop any conversions, especially to Christianity.

But Daniel continued to boldly preach the Gospel publicly. Angry, the militants plotted to attack him.

A few days later they surrounded his home and apprehended him as he was leaving the house. They beat him mercilessly. His wife heard his cries and ran to the door screaming for help. One of the attackers pushed her back into the house and locked the door from the outside. They continued beating Daniel until he lay senseless on the street in front of his house, badly battered.

None of these attacks discouraged Daniel as he continued to share Christ in the town. But his wife found it difficult to face the opposition and the scorn of her neighbors. She was often frightened, not only for herself, but for Daniel's safety, and after some months Anand suggested they move to another base.

Yet, there has been a breakthrough in this town that only a few years ago did not have one baptized believer. By 1983, three believers had taken baptism and two others were preparing for that important step.

The summer of 1978 brought intense heat—114 degrees in the shade, and drought. A bucket of water cost five rupees (fifty cents) in some towns. The teams stayed wherever they could find an available place. Sometimes all six crowded into a musty, airless room with cow dung or dirt floors, with roaches and other insects attacking them in the night. Often they were chased out to move on to another place when the landlord discovered what they were doing. Their reputation preceded them, and few Hindus would allow them to rent their property.

In spite of these harsh conditions, within one month the teams had visited over 12,000 homes. And requests for correspondence courses were coming in to RBI at the rate of 125 a day. Anand had not misinterpreted the spiritual hunger of the people.

Yet, he was perplexed. He wrote Allen Finley of *Christian Nationals* in July of 1978: "We have reached the bottom as far as finances are concerned. We are now holding all night prayer meetings, pleading with the Lord to help us in this situation."

Even with two large gifts of $6000 and $5000, the funds were soon depleted, for the printing bill was voracious. Anand wrote again, "We have been slow in providing the literature to our teams due to lack of enough funds. This is a great burden to carry."

As though Anand didn't have enough responsibility, RBI took over a high school in Jaipur that September. The Scottish Presbyterian Mission had established the Christian Mission School more than 100 years earlier. But when the missionaries left, they closed all their schools except this one, which was run by a local board. Now it was a crumbling building with no funds to operate it. The school officials urged Anand's board to take it over.

So in September 1978, the high school reopened with 187 students in the Hindi section, and 40 in the English. The school would eventually have more than 1000 children, and became self-supporting in three years through fees and scholarships. Many parents preferred sending their children to a Christian school, especially in the English medium, because of the high quality of education offered. So RBI began making a significant and much appreciated contribution to the people of Jaipur.

By October the teams were ready to come back to RBI for a period of training and rest. They'd been out in the towns for four long, hot months, and most had not seen their families during that period.

It was only when the teams arrived back on campus that the full impact of what was happening dawned on Anand and his staff.

As Anand listened to these young evangelists sitting cross-legged on the floor, singing and clapping their hands to the rhythm of the drum and the harmonium (a type of accordion), his heart swelled with joy. Most of the evangelists had little education—and little money. They were simple Indians who wore the hardships of pioneer evangelism as casually as their tattered shirts. Anand noticed the patch on Robert's trousers, and the holes in the toes of Joseph's socks. He knew most had left their wives and children behind in their home villages, and there was very little money to send back to them. But he never heard a word of complaint. Rather there was a great sense of excitement and joy as one by one they shared their experiences over the past months.

Robin Masih told about his team's visit to Alvur after they left Bharatpur. "We knew it was a stronghold of the Hindu community, but still, we felt that we must do the Lord's work here also. The first day we fasted and prayed and started the work. After we prayed we felt the fear of the people, and whatever danger there could be had been taken from our hearts . . . . Strangely, we found Muslims, Hindus, Sikhs and others eager to hear and know about the Lord

Jesus Christ."

Brother R. S. John, a Hindu convert, told of the experiences of his team in Ganganagar. "We were surprised that the people there didn't know what Christianity is. They wanted to know what a Christian costs."

One of the teams gained notoriety in the local RSS-sponsored newspaper after a van load of Christians from Jaipur had driven up to Chomu, a town just a little north of Jaipur, to help in some meetings. Neighbors reported their visit to the newspaper, which ran a story something like this:

> Christian preachers and workers started poisoning the whole atmosphere, and they are poisoning the minds of people . . . . The preacher who has been staying here in Chumo for the last few months has a tape recorder, a transistor radio, and seems to have quite a residence. He is spreading this Christianity here in Chumo. He is influencing the minds of our downtrodden classes and giving inducements of different kinds. Are these not agents of the CIA?

After this article appeared in the paper, the police visited Samuel who had made Chumo his base of residence.

They were blunt and to the point. "Why have you come here? Are the Americans paying you?"

Samuel, a wise and experienced evangelist, invited them in and carefully explained his purposé, glad for the open opportunity. "We are not supported by any government. People of God who are anxious that other people know about Him have provided our food and rent. Our main purpose is to tell you that it's because of sin that man is separated from God and the Gospel. Jesus Christ is the only way for a man to find the true God."

But they retorted, "Isn't is possible to have salvation through Hindu philosophies and practices? Our Hindu scriptures are older than yours. Why should a man worship only Christ?"

Brother Samuel reports, "I told them that the Lord Jesus says, 'I am the Way, the Truth and the Life,' and that He is the only way through which a man can get to God."

Even the ones who had reported the evangelist to the police came, initially to argue and cross-examine the Christians. But eventually they came back again and again to ask penetrating questions, and to listen to Brother Samuel's explanations. Though they did not accept Christ, they were no longer aggressive and opposing the evangelist in his work.

Sometimes Anand chuckled at the ingenuity of these young men. In Kushalgharh a group of young Communists accosted the team on the street, threatening to chase them out of town. While two of the team members engaged them in a long and serious discussion about party philosophy and Christian teaching, the others slipped away unnoticed and carried on distributing literature.

Two hours later they rejoined the team, having completed their assignment, to find the others still in deep discussion. Seeing their mates had returned, the leaders agreed that they would leave town and not distribute any more literature.

By the time the teams had completed the goals for Project 78, they had visited 250,000 homes, and more than 23,000 people had enrolled in the correspondence courses.

But what surprised Anand was that 6,000 of these students were women.

"This is the first time in my years of ministry that I saw women respond, openly write for correspondence courses, and indicate that they wanted to accept Christ," Anand explained.

Hindu women, especially in the villages, are still chattels of their husbands. As girls they are under their fathers' and brothers' domination. When they marry, they move to the control of their husbands' family. Though many of the educated women have responsible jobs, personal decisions, such as marriage and religion, are the family's responsibility. Few would dare to oppose them.

On the Sunday after the report about the women's response was received, Anand announced the results in the worship service at the Calvary Bible Church, on the grounds of RBI. As he spoke of the Hindu and Muslim women who were sharing the longings of their hearts, the past suddenly overwhelmed him. He could see his dear mother and little sister vainly prostrating themselves before the image of Durga, hoping their sacrifices and prayers would fulfill their karma and bring them another step closer to eternal oneness with nothingness.

They never heard what Jesus' love had done for them. For a moment Anand lost his composure as tears welled in his eyes.

Though his staff had heard his story, this was the first time they'd seen how deep the pain still was.

Later, in order to follow up these responses from women, Anand arranged for his sister-in-law, Kusum Jacob, who had earned her Master of Religious Education in Canada, to visit some of the women. But it was a hopeless task. Over and over she was greeted at the door by a brother or father of the girl who had written.

"Why do you want to see my sister? Are you a Christian?"

"Yes."

"Are you here to convert my sister to Christianity?"

Sometimes the mother would come to the door, angry and defiant. "Who do you think would marry my daughter if she becomes a Christian? We don't want you bothering her. Go away."

And the door would slam in her face.

Yet, over and over Anand would receive letters from women who had completed the correspondence course, or listened to his early morning radio Bible study, saying they had found Jesus to be true and wanted to accept Him as their Saviour. He could only trust that God's Spirit was witnessing to the hearts of these isolated babes in Christ who, behind the closed doors of their homes, were out of reach of the rest of the body.

Throughout the latter months of 1978 there were constant rumors of a new bill to be presented before Parliament—the Anti-Conversion Bill. A similar law had been passed in several of the states, but now it was threatening to become nationwide.

The Indian constitution guarantees "freedom of conscience and the right to freely profess, practise and propagate religion."

But the Anti-Conversion Bill would subtly undermine that freedom, for it would be illegal to use inducement, force, or threat of divine judgment to convert someone to another religion.

Could the offer of forgiveness, eternal life, and abundant joy be considered inducements? Would preaching hell and the wrath of God be interpreted as showing divine judgment? Christian leaders across the country recognized that a militant Hindu judge could misconstrue the facts. Or a convert's family could force him to admit pressure had been put on him to accept Christ.

Anand and his staff prayed much against it, realizing that it was already giving courage and motivation to militant Hindu groups. If it were passed, it could severely limit the work of evangelism.

So there was a greater sense of urgency about completing the visitation program in every town of Rajasthan. Even though funds were often slow in coming, and for a time printing had to be suspended, generous gifts continued to arrive through the efforts of *Christian Nationals.*

Early in 1979, Anand recruited another dozen evangelists, sending them out in newly reorganized teams. Some of the more experienced evangelists, like Brother Samuel, were sent to open permanent centers in places like Chomu and Sagwara—where there were no other Christian families, or to follow up responses from Project 78.

In the midst of endless activity and responsibility, Anand was grateful for the oasis of peace and contentment that his home, Sarla, and Pushbanjali provided. There were always extra people in and out. Their home was a center for many visitors. He missed Mother and Father Jacob—both had come to live with them in their last years, and had died within a year of each other. He missed the spiritual support of the long hours that Sarla's father had spent in prayer and fasting—a source of great strength to Anand.

Sarla missed her parents too, but she was glad to have one of her brothers in the work at RBI. Her sister, Kusum, had completed her studies in Canada and returned to work with women.

But Sarla worried about Anand. He seemed to be driven, and she feared that his health would break.

In four years the former home of the Maharajah's favorite dancer had become the center of a network of activities, with Anand at the hub.

Over thirty evangelists and church planters were out in the fields, while 24 staff members handled the thousands of letters and courses that came in each day. By the completion of Project 79, almost a million homes had been visited, and over 60,000 had enrolled in the correspondence courses.

During this same time, Anand was preparing nine weekly broadcasts and teaching the six original students. There were nine other students who had begun their Bachelor of Theology studies, and Anand himself completed his Bachelor of Divinity by correspondence. He pastored the Calvary Bible Church, meeting on the R.B.I. premises, which had over sixty people attending weekly, and he and the board were now operating two grade schools and one high school.

Meanwhile, Anand negotiated for building permits so that the Bible school could take in more students. A California church had promised funds for the first building. Anand filled out triplicate forms, but was shunted from office to office and waited in endless lines for permits that could have been granted easily if he'd been willing to make a "special gift."

At one point he wrote, "I am at a place where I feel so helpless and frustrated. I have to spend many hours in the government offices just to get a permit for a bag of cement. No one is willing to do anything unless he receives a bribe. If you don't pay them, you will get the same answer every day—come back tomorrow."

With all this rapid expanse, it's not surprising that the staff often wondered where Uncle Chaudhari was leading them, and if they could follow. "Sometimes he thinks so far ahead of us that we feel left behind," Regina confided. "It's confusing, with a ministry as wide-spread as ours, for one person to keep in touch with everything."

One of the main concerns for the staff was that Anand had no second in command when he would be away, or if something should happen to him. He seemed to find it hard to delegate responsibilities of leadership to them. As if to vindicate his reticence, one of Anand's trusted workers was found to have mismanaged funds. In retrospect, Anand believes this was one of the most serious mistakes of judgment he made. "I didn't really wait upon the Lord whether I should take this man and give him such responsibility. From the beginning he was doing things behind my back to malign my leadership and poison the people against me."

Anand found it difficult to ask the man to leave, and the months of suspicion and doubt took its toll on the staff. Morale was at its lowest ebb when the culprit was finally sent away.

Even overseas supporters were adding pressure. From Canada Dr. Doxsee complained, "One church in the States is quite dissatisfied with no communications or regular letters, which are a must if you do not want to lose support." In the midst of these increasing burdens, Anand began experiencing excruciating headaches. He finally took Sarla's advice to go to a doctor, who found his blood pressure had soared.

"You'll have to take at least a fortnight's rest, or this could kill you," his doctor warned. But this was more than a doctor's prescription. God used the enforced rest to touch Anand's life so that he returned to his duties with renewed zeal.

It was in those days that Regina's monthly report to prayer partners expressed these words of promise by Elsie Campbell, which echoed Anand's experience:

I tried to lift a heavy load—
I thought my back would surely break
Until I called a Friend
Some of the weight for Him to take—
and then between us, easily
We bore the load too much for me.

Yet none of the problems troubled Anand as much as the fact that with all the responses to radio and correspondence courses, with all the letters confessing Christ as Lord, there were no baptisms. Taking a public stand of baptism was a difficult and costly step, and in the eyes of the Hindu community the ultimate break with Hinduism. Until believers were ready to follow the Lord in baptism, there would be no new churches in Rajasthan. And it was the Church that God had in mind when He picked Anand out of the thousands of students at the University of Bombay and put him on a debating team with a Christian.

Anand entered 1981 with a heavy heart.

15

Faith Stretched Again

By mid-1981, Anand had worked through about half of the Old Testament on his daily radio broadcast, ARADHANA (WORSHIP), over Trans World Radio. Dr. J. Vernon McGee, beloved American Bible teacher, had not only given permission to use the basic materials of his well-known series, *Thru the Bible,* but was helping to finance the daily broadcasts.

The medium wave signal from Sri Lanka was strong enough to be heard in most of India, and Anand was receiving letters from all over the country. At one point the staff counted 6000 communities from which listeners had written.

One morning as Anand was preparing his program from the book of Esther, the Word of God jumped off the pages to strike his own heart. In the face of impending disaster, Esther told Mordecai, "Go, gather all the Jews to be found in Susa, and hold a fast on my behalf. Neither eat nor drink for three days, night or day. I and my maids will also fast as you do" (Esther 4:16).

Even as Anand recorded the radio message on how Esther found an answer to her problem, God was convicting him that he must follow her example. That day, as soon as the recording was completed, he left the studio and went in to speak to his staff.

"The Lord has shown me that we should stop our work for three days and spend the time in fasting and praying. We need His presence in a new way here in the office. We need His healing and refreshing Spirit to fall upon us. Then we can expect Him to touch our converts and give them courage to follow Him in baptism."

The very first morning of fasting and prayer a spirit of revival broke out. As one staff member after another poured out his heart to God, each sensed His cleansing and peace. Hurts of the past months were healed.

God spoke so vividly that the three days became a turning point for the ministry. From that time on Anand scheduled regular days of fasting and prayer.

In one of these later times of fasting, God did a miracle in the life of Nathanael, whose beautiful voice was heard regularly on ARADHANA. No one listening to him sing could imagine that Nathanael could not speak one sentence without stammering. The staff had been praying for his healing ever since he'd joined RBI.

But during one special day of prayer, Nathanael began praising God and confessing his sin, and miraculously he was able to do so without a struggle. Now he praises God with his voice and his words.

Just a few weeks after the periods of fasting and prayer, news came that some converts in Jodhpur had requested baptism. This ancient Rajasthan city of half a million had heard the Gospel long ago, but most of its churches were dead. Anand had sent Brother Vijay Singh, a weathered evangelist, to work among the non-churched Hindus of Jodhpur. Reports began coming back of conversions.

Finally, Brother Singh asked Anand to come and baptize seventeen new converts—the breakthrough was made. Before the year was out more than eighty-five people had been baptized from Jodhpur and surrounding areas, and a church of over fifty Hindu converts was meeting regularly.

In Jaipur the touch of God was also felt. In the beginning Anand had started Sunday worship for the institute students and staff. At first they met in the office, but that soon became too small, for some forty new converts had also joined the congregation, now called Calvary Church.

So a large colorful tent was erected on the open ground inside the wall. And that was soon full of desks and chairs during the week, as correspondence course markers increased to keep up with the more than 48,000 students enrolled.

One young man, Samuel Chota, who attended Calvary Church, was so small in stature that he laughingly joked about himself, "I could have easily been named Zacchaeus."

Samuel was born in the eastern state of Orissa in a tribal home. Though most tribals are animists, he remembers studying the religious books of Hinduism, even as a child. When he was eighteen he met a Christian who shared the New Testament with him. "I compared the Hindu scriptures and the Bible, and had to accept that Jesus alone promised to give eternal life. I stood before the Saviour of this world, and could not help but accept Him as mine."

But when he went home and told his parents they were enraged. "I received a good thrashing for my first step into Christianity, and they threw me out of the house."

Over the years God cared for Samuel, putting him in touch with Christians who helped him study and serve the Lord. But while he was in Jaipur, the Lord burdened him for his family back in Orissa, whom he'd not seen for many years.

One day Samuel came to Anand's office to share his concern. "Uncle, I must go back to Orissa to tell my own people about Christ."

Anand presented Chota's plan to the small body of believers in Jaipur, and they joyfully decided to send him as their missionary.

Chota's home was in a difficult mountainous area, and the tribal people were fierce and dangerous. Only someone from the tribe could safely work among them. In order to help him get around to isolated villages, Calvary Church sent him money for a bicycle.

Chota's sense of humor was a great asset in that difficult place of ministry. He wrote back to the church, "In some places the road is so bad I have to carry my cycle and walk. So you see, sometimes the cycle carries me, and at other times I carry the cycle."

Within the first year Chota was able to lead his parents to become Christians, and he was even able to marry a Christian girl. When Calvary Church wrote to offer an increase in his allowance, he replied, "What I receive is enough, please do not think of giving me more. If you want to give, then give me another worker; support him so that he can work along with me."

The church did just that, and a second worker joined Samuel in that desperately poor mountainous area, among the illiterate tribals about whom it is said, "They never smile."

That Christmas Samuel took his Christmas gift from the church and constructed a mud and thatch building for his new little group of believers.

Back in Jaipur the urgency for more buildings for RBI increased. There wasn't room for more than fifteen or eighteen students in the converted stable, which had once housed the horses of the maharajah's favorite dancer. A hostel was desperately needed as living quarters for students. After three years of scorching heat, wind and monsoon rains, the tent was showing signs of deterioration. Though funds had been promised from overseas, and radio listeners were sending about $1000 a month for the work from India itself, the RBI staff was stymied for lack of a building permit.

The excuses of the officials were just that—excuses.

"Fill in another form . . . . You'll need the signature of the superintendent . . . . He won't be back until next week . . . . Come back tomorrow . . . . We have to get permission from higher authorities."

Anand was well aware that an offer of a bribe to the right party would take care of all the objections—but he refused to pay it.

So often the permit approval seemed so close that Anand and his workers were sure it would be only a matter of weeks before they would be building. Early in 1982 the way seemed clear. The final approval lay on the desk of the minister in Jaipur, just waiting for his signature.

But once again months passed and nothing happened. Anand made frequent trips to the office. It was suggested to Anand, "If you can give us a little something, we'll see that it gets to his attention right away." The "little something" suggested amounted to about $5000.

Yet in faith the staff continued to pray and believe. They believed enough to have building plans for the hostel and classrooms drawn. There were at least 100 qualified student applicants in the files waiting to be accepted by the institute. And with the number of house churches starting (the goal of fifty house fellowships by 1985 was reached two years ahead of schedule) the need for trained Hindi speaking Bible teachers and church planters was becoming desperate.

By now, replacing the tent was an urgent and immediate need. Anand decided they would put up a temporary shed on the site of the future chapel. It seemed only logical to pour the foundations which could then be used for a permanent building later on.

Once that was done, it made sense to pour the slab floor.

Why not just put the walls up since they had funds in hand? Even without asking for donations, hundreds of their radio friends included small love gifts to help with the cost of the ministry when they wrote their letters. That money had been accumulating for just such an emergency as this.

So the building went up like "topsy"—without specific plans or permission.

But they couldn't expect to build in as conspicuous a place as this without coming to the attention of the local authorities.

One day a city official arrived, bristling with indignation.

"We have no record for a permit for this building," he accused.

Anand had his answer ready. "But this is a holy place, sir. As you can see, we had no place of worship here."

The official's face dropped and he looked embarrassed. "Well, if it's a temple it's all right."

The unwritten law of India is that no temple may be desecrated or torn down, nor is permission needed to build one. "Theoretically, you could build a temple in the middle of the road, and it would have to honored and protected," Anand explained.

By taking advantage of this loophole, an attractive chapel seating over 200 people was completed, not looking like "topsy" at all. Later an adjoining room was built which is being used as a library and classroom. But without additional hostels they could still not increase the student body.

Anand spent many hours in prayer over this need. He admitted he was perplexed at God's "inaction" when everything else pointed to the need for a larger seminary.

The vast scope of what God was doing through his radio ministry really only hit Anand as he began moving out to hold meetings in other areas where radio responses were most concentrated. In some towns he found that small house churches had sprung up where there had never been an evangelist or missionary. Family groups and neighbors had simply begun gathering to listen to the radio teaching and worship together.

In February 1982, Anand went to Nagpur to hold a city-wide campaign. He expected 300-400 people. The meeting was held outdoors, and the first evening there were more than 3000 attending. When he asked, "How many listen to our radio broadcast every day?" a sea of hands rose. The warmth of response was overwhelming. After the meeting many came to say, "We feel like you are part of our family."

Others made themselves known in the least expected places. One night Anand had a reservation in a sleeping compartment on the night train for Delhi. As he entered the four-berth compartment, his three other traveling companions were already seated. As is the custom on Indian trains, he began to introduce himself to the others.

One of the men interrupted him, "You don't have to introduce yourself. We know who you are. We recognize your voice."

Anand learned that the three men were scientists who had just returned from an interview with Prime Minister Indira Gandhi.

"We hear your program every morning. In fact, you can hear the program throughout our whole colony (housing complex)."

Before they reached their destination the men invited Anand to visit them and explain more about the Bible.

On another train journey there was confusion about bookings, and Anand found there was no record of his reservation—a must if you want to be sure of a seat on a train in India.

Suddenly an elderly man seated in the waiting room called him over and invited him to join him in his first class compartment.

After they were settled on the train, the man volunteered, "I suppose you're wondering why I invited you into my compartment." Anand nodded and waited for the explanation.

"It's because I hear you on the radio every morning—I recognized your voice as you spoke to the station master. I want to know about that peace you always talk about. I do want what you have."

Far into the night Anand explained the story of Jesus to this man, whom he'd learned was a Hindu professor of philosophy at a leading Indian university. Anand could see the professor's heart respond as he told once again of the wonderful perfection and purity of Jesus Christ who had drawn him out of darkness.

At two o'clock in the morning, the professor knelt on the floor of the rolling train and prayed, "Lord Jesus, I want you to give me the same assurance of sins forgiven as this man has."

As the two men parted the next morning the professor testified, "I really feel something has changed me." He urged Anand to visit him when he came back to Delhi. But when Anand later went to his home some months later, he learned that the professor had died suddenly of a heart attack.

Even as the Word of God was going out in power through radio, correspondence courses, church planters and campaigns, Anand felt a disturbing attack of the devil upon the ministry.

The stagnation of organization can be insidious. He noticed that some of his workers began to find fault with him and his programs. Not that they said much to him. The Indian man finds it difficult to confront, especially an elder or one in authority over him.

But rumor came to him that some workers were complaining

about his leadership and felt they wanted to have a greater voice in decision making.

Some felt he gave his family too many privileges. They were jealous of his opportunities to contact overseas donors, and of the benefits that accrued as a result. Even the car the Bingleys had provided for him became a source of irritation—though they didn't know that the Bingleys had given money twice and Anand had simply used the money for the work, rather than honoring his "parents" request.

The bitterness finally erupted when one of the original students left to join another ministry, dividing the loyalties of the rest of the staff, and causing Anand deep heartache.

Yet Anand defends his style of leadership from his own experience. "From the beginning God has led me very clearly step-by-step.

"I gave away my father's property at the distinct instructions from the Word of God.

"I went to the Jhansi Bible School at His direct guidance. I could have ended up at a liberal seminary or even with some strange sect. I knew nothing of the differences in Christianity at that time.

"God's leading has been a guiding principle in all of my ministry. I take the steps in the direction I feel the Lord is leading me, regardless of the consequences.

"When I've done this, the Lord has taken care and seen that plans have come to fruition. I'm not afraid to step out on faith, even when there is no evidence of funds or people to fulfill the plan."

There's a note of sadness in his voice as he explains, "My own people don't understand why I think so big. They worry about how this or that is going to happen without funds. But I've seen that as I take a step, somehow the funds are always there. If I had held back because of others' fears, we wouldn't be in the place where we are now.

"When we started we had nothing. Yet even when we bought this property I simply acted on God's clear leading, though I didn't have $100 to my name."

Anand's unusual manner of leadership which excites either fierce loyalty or resentment in his followers, grows out of his lifelong practice of meditation on the Scriptures and prayer.

"When an idea comes into my mind, I seclude myself with the Scriptures and pray about it until I have perfect peace in my heart that the Lord has guided me.

"Not all of my colleagues here are with me. Some blindly follow me saying, 'Whatever Uncle is thinking must be all right.' Some are skeptical; some only think in their own terms—'What if everything collapses?' So they are scared.

"I do share with them and ask for prayer. My board is very helpful and I never make major changes without consulting with them first. But I feel very definitely that I have to take responsibility for the final decision."

In many ways Anand is still the loner of his youth. Very few realize how much he depends upon Sarla to listen, comfort and understand as he serves with single-minded purpose.

When he walks into the house, she's invariably there to tend to his needs. Often without voicing them, she senses his wishes and places a glass of cold water or a welcome cup of tea in his hands. She alone knows how to read the weariness in his face, the grief over disappointments, and the financial burdens resting on his shoulders.

Anand's and Sarla's mutual love and parental concern center on Pinkie, who has grown into a striking young woman. Even as a teenager, she wears her brilliant saris with exquisite grace. She experiments with her heavy hair which reaches almost to her waist— sometimes flowing freely in a silky black cloud around her heart-shaped face, or piled in innocent sophistication on her head.

When Pinkie sings in her lilting soprano, Anand's eyes light up with special warmth reserved only for her. But at home she often flits silently through the rooms, a private person, much like her father.

Anand may sometimes wonder about what direction his reserved young daughter's life may take, but he has a clear picture in his mind as to what His Lord wants him to do. God has given him an uncanny organizational ability to implement his vision. He can use simple village evangelists with little training, and yet inspire them to visit contacts systematically, send regular reports, and establish house churches.

Anand has the ability to keep many projects on track at the same time, keeping one hand on details, while with the other painting the big picture. He has an amazing ability to follow through; when he sets goals they are almost invariably met.

Some leaders of the Indian church aren't sure they understand Anand. He wants to cooperate with other evangelicals, but if they refuse, it does not deter him from following his own vision, even if he has to go it alone. He has closed schools and moved evangelists if he felt they would compete with existing ministries. When one evangelical leader accused him of placing follow-up workers where he wanted to work, Anand simply said, "Tell me where you want to go and I'll put my workers elsewhere. If we had 1000 follow-up workers for India, it wouldn't be enough."

He admits that visions can change. "I believe God sometimes gives a vision for a short time, and when His goal is met, He stops that and directs me to another one."

Anand is a tireless worker, driving himself long hours, filling schedules with speaking engagements. In spite of this, he takes time to officiate at a staff wedding or share in an engagement party. Around the RBI campus he mixes with visitors, who are constantly coming and going, quietly slipping in and out like a doctor on his rounds, never giving indication of the pressures or burdens he's carrying.

Even so, Anand often records several radio messages in one day, since tapes must be to the station three months in advance. When he is going to be away from RBI for several weeks or months, he may prepare ten to fifteen in one stretch. His gift of study, interpretation and retention enable him to perform this almost superhuman task.

Family loyalties are very important to Anand. Ever since the Jacob family befriended him and took him in as a son, he has loved them as his own. One or two of Sarla's brothers and sisters have always lived with them, and he has helped educate them. Sarla's parents spent the last years of their lives with them. Traditionally, Indian sons are expected to care for their families, and Anand feels that this was his responsibility.

But more than that, he sees in the Jacobs' children the products of godly, praying parents. Every one of the eight children is a Christian, and most are in Christian service. Quiet and humble, they evidence integrity and commitment—qualities not easily found, even in trained Christian workers.

It is through Sarla's brother, Anil, that one of the most exciting recent breakthroughs has come.

In 1981, Anil left his job in Allahabad to join Anand in Rajasthan. He had been in secular work for some time, but he wanted to serve the Lord on a full-time basis. At this time Anand was looking for evangelists to put into outlying areas to follow up radio contacts. One group that was beginning to show unusual interest was the primitive Bhil tribe in western Rajasthan, which numbered about two million.

When Anil agreed to work among the Bhils, he knew it would not be easy. In the mountainous interior regions, many of the people still live naked, using Stone Age tools, and resorting to violence and murder to settle their differences.

But with the help of two young Bhil evangelists, Anil was able to survey the entire region and found the people ready to listen. Since most were illiterate, he taught them Scripture through songs which the people readily learned by rote.

In February 1983, Anand and several from Jaipur went to Chittargarh for the first Bhil convention organized by the tribal workers. They watched amazed as people streamed down the rugged mountain paths, some walking more than thirty-five miles for the meetings. The first night, 1500 people sat under the starry Indian sky listening to Anand teach the Scriptures.

Later during the conference, Anand baptized thirty-three converts. Within another year, more than two hundred would be baptized and eight house churches formed.

This tribe, which has for generations rebuffed any attempts of evangelization, is now on the verge of a mass conversion, with whole families and villages becoming Christians. Anand knew that if the Holy Spirit continued to spearhead this movement, it could sweep through the entire tribe. His heart was overawed!

16
The Vision Never Ends

Madhurani's tears splashed into the glass. "Just a minute, Ranu. Mummy's getting you some milk," she called in a voice quivering with emotion.

Her two little girls, six and eight, were curled up on mats on the dirt floor, ready to go to sleep. Her body ached from moving rocks on the road today, but at least she'd been able to purchase a jug of milk on the way home. The girls loved a warm cup before they went to sleep.

Madhurani sighed heavily and wiped the tears off her bruised cheek. In his drunken stupor, her husband, Laschni, had beaten her almost senseless before he'd left to drive a truck last night. She'd only begged him for food money, but as so many times in the past, he'd spent his week's wages on drink. Her pleas fell on besotted ears.

She reached into the folds of her sari for the crumpled packet she'd purchased with her last rupee. A few grains of the powder in the milk would be enough—then she and the girls would never be hungry or beaten again. Perhaps in the next life the gods would be merciful.

As she struggled to open the packet with her shaking hands, Ranu called again, and suddenly Madhurani fell to the floor weeping. She couldn't do it—not tonight.

"I woke early the next morning, confused and angry that I had lost my courage," Madhurani wrote to Anand. "My husband's radio was sitting on the table. I turned it on and heard your program. You had such a message of hope and peace, it was just as though you were speaking to me."

After listening for several mornings, Madhurani knelt before the radio and gave her life to Jesus. When her husband returned from his truck driving job, he was angry and beat her. "I won't have you listening to a Christian program!" Undaunted, Madhurani kept urging him to listen too. Finally, he also became a Christian, and both were baptized. No longer would Madhurani wish to die; her husband had become a new person in Christ.

Such stories thrilled Anand. Over and over he read of Hindus and Muslims saved through listening to ARADHANA. The fact that so many women wrote in response to the program continued to touch his heart.

By September 1984, Anand completed preaching through the entire Bible. TWR considered changing the format, and Anand felt that perhaps he should broaden his exposure.

While TWR had an estimated listening audience of five million, the most popular shortwave station in the country, Radio Ceylon, claimed one hundred million listeners.

And now he had the opportunity to buy time and broadcast the Gospel over this powerful secular station. Because Radio Ceylon did not schedule Christian programs back-to-back, listeners who'd tuned in for news and rock often heard him preach.

Early in 1985, Anand began broadcasting a daily ten-minute program on the promises of God over Radio Ceylon. Within a few months he was astonished to see 75 to 100 letters arrive each day.

Between the two stations, responses poured in from all over North India, an area with twice the population of the United States. Even though RBI evangelists worked in eleven states, they could not possibly follow up those who wrote for spiritual help from all 220 districts of this vast area.

Anand was overwhelmed.

What really discouraged him was the spiritual vaccuum new converts lived in. For example, a Sikh mother who appeared at RBI one morning typified needs of these inquirers. She and her two daughters took their radio out in the front yard every morning to listen secretly. As a zealous Sikh, her husband strongly opposed their interest, but he could not stop their faith

Now on a family visit to the Punjab, the mother and her daughters stopped at RBI. "Brother Chaudhari, we want to be baptized. Teach us about God's Word. What does Jesus mean by 'living water'? How can He be the truth, the way, and the life all at the same time? How does the Holy Spirit comfort?" Once they returned home, they would not find any other Christians.

In the face of hundreds like this Sikh woman, Anand's spirits sank. How could they be fed and nurtured? Even if RBI could fund workers in each area, they would still not be enough.

By now it was obvious to Anand that his ministry had extended far beyond the boundaries of Rajasthan. Against his personal inclinations for privacy and time to study, it became clear that expansion of the RBI facilities, the follow-up staff, the evangelists, and every phase of the work has to occur.

"I know God is leading me. But I personally would not have chosen these administrative responsibilities," Anand states categorically.

Now in his 55th year, Anand craves time to study and write. He recognizes the tremendous need for Hindi Christian literature, a task for which he is so eminently qualified. Yet how can he turn his back on the desperate need for trained leaders? He has to choose.

For the first time, in talking about the vast opportunities waiting to be tackled, Anand admits to the loneliness of being on the top, of having to make major decisions which will again call on every ounce of energy and every resource he possesses.

"I don't have anyone at the moment with whom I can really share my vision . . . I'm longing for someone to take over my administrative work. I've finally learned not to worry about it anymore. God has taught me that it's His work, not mine."

Anand cannot wait for someone to come along and help him bear the load. As he reads the increasing volume of letters, he understands that most of his listeners are writing out of a background of hopeless heathenism. They have no churches to attend, no Christian friends, no literature. And sadly, the few churches in these areas usually do not welcome Hindu converts with warmth and love.

Pushing his human weariness and sense of heavy burden aside, Anand opens the Scriptures, where he has always found God's guidance for his dilemma.

And God does not fail.

As Anand ponders the Scriptures, he also gets out his beloved maps. He often pores over them to claim different areas of India for God. For so long Rajasthan has been his prime target. But now as he studies his maps again, the Lord seems to be saying, "North India— with its 450 million people."

Then as he meditates and prays, that clear vision from God, which he has experienced so often before, washes over his soul, and the maps before him vibrate. They become God's blueprint.

Possibilities reshape themselves to form concrete ideas.

"We could develop prayer fellowships as nurturing groups," he says half aloud.

Anand leans back in his chair, his expressive fingers resting on his lips as God crystallizes his vision.

"I'll use our Prayer Fellowship magazine to provide Bible study material," he muses. The inexpensive little monthly paper is already going out to more than 14,000 people with prayer requests sent in by radio listeners. Now he will add simple Bible studies so that new believers could use them on their own.

Anand spins around in his chair to look out towards the gate where noisy throngs are passing. In place of the heavy burden of finding enough trained workers to meet the needs of India's masses, Anand begins to sense clear direction and hope.

It seems as though the Lord is whispering, "If you will take this next step of faith and trust me to enable you, I will use you and your workers to plant one thousand churches all across North India in the next five years. Trust me and do it."

Anand relaxes. Once again he experiences the presence of the King of his life, the One whose royal son he'd become on the seashore that January evening in Bombay thirty years earlier.

God has led him through deep waters, but never too deep.

He has given him big vision, but never too big.

He has taken all that was dear, but never too much.

He has given him a lonely place of leadership, but He is always with him.

If only he could see his father, the "Shastri," once more. He would greet him as a son should, falling on his knees to touch his father's feet. He would assure him, "Father, I have honored your promise. I've served God—the only true God—with all of my being. He has blessed me far beyond your deepest desires, for I was destined to serve the King of kings."

Epilogue

The thud of hammers and falling bricks reverberated in the early morning air. Brick by brick, the old stables which served as a dormitory shuddered into oblivion. Women stooped to fill their basins with the dusty refuse, and place them on their heads. The mind-deadening labor was nevertheless welcome. There would be rupees and food for their children tonight.

To Anand, watching the last vestiges of the ancient buildings disappear, this marked the end of an era. He had closed the old Rajasthan Bible Institute at the end of 1986.

But this closing resembled a moth in a cocoon, waiting for new life and new form to emerge. With the approval of the building plans, construction would at least begin on the new RBI. It had taken ten years of patient waiting and dreaming.

The decision to close down the school in the intermin had not come easily. Disappointed with young leaders in whom he'd invested a great deal of training, Anand was forced to start over with new leadership. His perseverance paid off. Now he broadcasts twice daily—once over Trans World Radio, and once over Sri Lanka's commercial radio station. As the responses mushroom, Anand identifies a growing hunger to know Christ.

With well over 115 evangelists and church planters stationed across this sea of 450 million souls, Anand wants to provide periods of training geared to their immediate situations. He'd learned that highly trained leaders, weaned from the rigors of village life, find it difficult ever to go back to the isolation and simplicity of living with villagers.

When the building is completed, it will house over 100 students, who will take courses for six to nine months, and return to their fields of service for a year, before studying again.

Today more than 60 churches have been planted in Rajasthan and other parts of North India, and over 250 prayer fellowships started. Anand believes God is at last fulfilling the vision he'd been given when he first came to the land of the Rajahs.

Glossary of Indian Terms

Bhagavad-gita—An epic Hindu poem containing the stories of Krishna.

Brahman—The supreme Hindu spirit.

Brahmin—Priest or highest caste.

Chapati—Thin, flat, round unleavened bread, similar to a tortilla.

Dhoti—Cloth wrapped around a man's waist reaching to his knees.

Durga—Hindu goddess, wife of Shiva and mother of the elephant-headed god, Ganesha. Durga is a symbol of power and protection.

Ghee—Clarified butter used in worship.

Harijan—"Children of God"—name given to outcastes or untouchables by Mahatma Gandhi.

Kali—Mother goddess of destruction after whom the city of Calcutta was named.

Karma—Retribution for accumulated good and evil of each mortal lifetime which determines whether a soul migrates up or down. Hindus must humbly accept their lot in order to assure a better destiny in the next life.

Krishna—Incarnation of the god Vishnu.

Kshatriya—Warrior caste.

Mantra—Verse of Hindu scripture which is believed to have power when offered as a prayer.

Mata—Hindu goddess of smallpox also known as Sitala.

Naman—Two parallel lines of white drawn on a priest's head from hairline to eyebrows; a third red line is drawn parallel between them.

Panchayat—Informal court made up of leaders of the caste community.

Puja—Ritual sacrifices of worship

Ramayana—Epic poem, part of Hindu scriptures.

Sadhu—Holy ascetics who beg for a living.

Shastras—Sacred books of Hinduism.

Shastri—Hindu priest who has mastered the Hindu scriptures; the diminutive, shastriji, is a special term of respect of a shastri.

Shiva—One of a triumverate of Hindu gods, known as the destroyer.

Sudra—Artisan or craftsmen caste.

Vaisyas—Trader or business caste.

Upanishads—Hindu scriptures.

Upanayana—Ceremony in which a young Brahmin receives sacred cord; a rite of passage.

Veda—Hindu scriptures.

A WORD FROM CHRISTIAN NATIONALS EVANGELISM COMMISSION

Anand Chaudhari's call, unique gifts, and single-minded dedication to making Christ known had one serious limitation. His support base in India was too small and too poor to implement the vision God had given him to do. Anand's contact and subsequent affiliation with CHRISTIAN NATIONALS was just one more step in the sovereign plan of God to build His church in north India.

CHRISTIAN NATIONALS was born out of a vision to help national Christian workers. In 1943 a group of Christian business-men in the Pacific Northwest formed a committee to assist indigen-ous evangelists in Mainland China. Before the Communist victory in 1950, the Chinese Native Evangelistic Crusade (CNEC), as it was then known, was assisting 129 evangelists and had helped plant thirteen churches, two Bible colleges, and a nationwide student movement.

When refugees poured out of China to Hong Kong and Singapore, CHRISTIAN NATIONALS was ready to assist Chinese leaders there in planting churches and relieving suffering. As fellowship and partnership with developing national leadership grew, ministries were added in Malaysia, Singapore, Thailand, the Philippines, etc.

Today CHRISTIAN NATIONALS assists eighty independent national ministries in some forty countries. About 1600 national workers are associated with these programs of evangelism, church planting, leadership training, education, relief and development. For example, Evangelist Siodora leads the Philippine Missionary Fel-lowship, with almost 150 Filipino missionaries working in unreached villages of this island nation. Without the help of CHRISTIAN NATIONALS partners, PMF would not have been able to add more missionaries, though scores had applied. With the call for 200,000 missionaries by the year 2000, in order to reach the world's unreached people, CHRISTIAN NATIONALS believes the growing force of Third World missions will play a vital role. These national workers know the language and culture, can live in the lifestyle of the local people, and require far less financial support than most Westerners.

If you would like further information about how you can join in partnership with nationals like Anand Chaudhari, write:

CHRISTIAN NATIONALS
International Headquarters
Box 15025
San Jose, CA 95115-0025

Partners International
A ministry of CHRISTIAN NATIONALS
1470 N. 4th St.
San Jose, CA 95112

CHRISTIAN NATIONALS
P.O. Box 67
Croydon Park
N. W. W. 2133
Australia

CHRISTIAN NATIONALS
2110 Argentia Rd. St. 308
Mississauga, ON L5N 2AK7
Canada

CHRISTIAN NATIONALS
Inage-Park-House A705
1223-I Sonnou-cho
Chiba-Shi 281
Japan

CHRISTIAN NATIONALS
11 Kildare Avenue
St. Heliers
Auckland 5
New Zealand

CHRISTIAN NATIONALS
Wangey Road
Chadwell Heath
Essex RM6 4DB

1989

Trinity Wesleyan H Wl

Bed Foster	8-4-89
Mildred Hays	8-15-89
Kennith Cobb	8-31-89
Marie Cobb	8-31-89
Ruth Putnam	10-15-89